To

_____

From

_____

Date

_____

Morning by Morning

© 2005 Christian Art Gifts, RSA
Christian Art Gifts Inc., IL, USA

Designed by Christian Art Gifts

Printed in China

ISBN 978-1-86920-544-7

09 10 11 12 13 14 15 16 17 18 – 17 16 15 14 13 12 11 10 9 8

ONE-MINUTE DEVOTIONS

MORNING
BY
MORNING

Charles Spurgeon

christian
art gifts®

JANUARY

THE PROMISED REST

That year they ate of the produce of Canaan.
Joshua 5:12

Our "promised rest" is to be with Jesus. If we are living by faith, that prospect should fill us with joy. The Holy Spirit is the down payment on our inheritance. To those who believe, He gives a foretaste of heavenly glory.

Heaven is a place of security; but we on earth are kept safe in Jesus. Heaven is a place of triumph; but we have victories, too. Those in heaven enjoy communion with the Lord; but this is not denied to us. They rest in His love, but we also have perfect peace in Him. They sing His praises; and it is our privilege to bless Him, too.

In all these ways in this coming year, we will gather celestial fruits on earthly ground. Faith and hope have turned this desert into the garden of God.

DEVOTE YOURSELVES TO PRAYER

JANUARY 2

*Devote yourselves to prayer,
being watchful and thankful.*
Colossians 4:2

It is interesting to note how much of Scripture is concerned with the subject of prayer, in furnishing examples, enforcing precepts, or pronouncing promises. We can be sure that whatever God has made prominent in His Word He wants to be conspicuous in our lives.

A prayerless soul is a Christless soul. Prayer is the lisping of the believing infant, the shout of the fighting believer, the requiem of the dying saint falling asleep in Jesus. It is the breath, the watchword, the comfort, the strength, the honor of a Christian. If you are God's child, you will seek your Father's face and live in your Father's love. The motto for this year must be "Devote yourselves to prayer."

CHRIST OUR COVENANT

*I will keep you and will make you
to be a covenant for the people.*
Isaiah 49:8

Jesus Christ is the sum and substance of the covenant. As a gift of the covenant, He is the property of every believer. All that Christ, as God and Man, ever had or will have is yours – from God's free favor, to be your inheritance forever.

Our blessed Jesus, as God, is omniscient, omnipresent, omnipotent. All that Jesus has as perfect man is yours. As a perfect man, Jesus enjoyed the Father's perfect delight. He stood accepted by the Most High God. Believer, God's acceptance of Christ is your acceptance. Don't you know that the love the Father bestowed on Christ He is bestowing on you now? For all that Christ did is yours. That perfect righteousness that Jesus worked out through His stainless life is yours; it is credited to your account.

GROW IN GRACE

But grow in the grace and knowledge
of our Lord and Savior Jesus Christ.
2 Peter 3:18

We should be growing in every aspect of our Lord's grace. That means growing in faith, the root of grace. Let your faith grow fuller, steadier, and simpler. Grow also in love. Ask God to make your love more extensive, more intense, more practical. Grow in humility as well. As you grow downward in humility seek also to grow upward, growing closer to God in prayer.

May God's Holy Spirit also enable you to "grow in the ... knowledge of our Lord and Savior." We should seek to know more of Jesus, more of His divine nature, His human relationships, His finished work of salvation, His death and resurrection, His present intercession for us, and His future return as King.

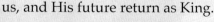

LIGHT AND DARKNESS

God saw that the light was good,
and he separated the light from the darkness.
Genesis 1:4

When the Holy Spirit gives us spiritual light, opening our eyes to behold the glory of God in the face of Jesus Christ, we see sin in its true colors and ourselves in our real position. Spiritual light has many beams and prismatic colors – knowledge, joy, holiness, and life. All are divinely good.

Light and darkness have no communion with each other. God divided them; we must not confuse them.

In judgment, in action, in hearing, in teaching, in association, we must discern between the precious and the vile, maintaining that great distinction the Lord made on the world's first day.

GOD CARES FOR YOU

JANUARY 6

Cast all your anxiety on him because he cares for you.
1 Peter 5:7

It soothes our sorrow when we realize, He cares for me. Christian, how can you dishonor your faith by looking so worried all the time? Cast your burden upon your Lord. Child of suffering, be patient. God has not passed over you. He who feeds sparrows will furnish you with what you need. Do not let despair drag you down; hope, always hope.

There is One who cares for you. Do not doubt God's grace when you face trouble. Believe that He loves you just as much in tough times as in happy times. If you trust Him with your soul, why not trust Him with your body as well? Leave your concerns in the hands of a gracious God.

TO LIVE IS CHRIST

For to me, to live is Christ.
Philippians 1:21

A person begins to live for Christ when the Holy Spirit convinces him of his sin and when by grace he sees the Savior's sacrifice cleansing his guilt. For believers, Jesus is the "pearl of great price" (Mt. 13:45-46), for whom we are willing to part with all we have. He has completely won our love; our hearts beat only for Him.

For His glory we live; for His gospel we would die. He is the pattern of our life; we sculpt our character with Him as our model.

Many of us live for Christ, somewhat. But who can truly say that he lives totally for Jesus? Yet Jesus is our life – its source and sustenance. The way we live, our purpose, all rolled into one name: Christ Jesus.

SACRED GIFTS

He will bear the guilt involved in the sacred gifts.
Exodus 28:38

Our "sacred gifts" contain far more guilt than we would think. The "guilt" involved in our public worship – the hypocrisy, irreverence, wandering of heart. Or consider our work for the Lord – its selfishness and carelessness. Or our private devotions – their laxity, coldness and neglect. Even our desires for holiness may be polluted by wrong motives. Worms hide under the greenest sods; we don't need to look very long to find them.

   It is encouraging to note that the high priest, bearing the guilt of the sacred gifts, wore a turban that bore these words, "Holy to the Lord." In the same way, Jesus bears our sin, presenting to the Father not our unholiness, but His own holiness.

ALL YOU NEED

I will be their God.
Jeremiah 31:33

Christian, here is all you need. You want something that satisfies; isn't this enough? If you could pour this promise into a cup, wouldn't you say with David, "My cup overflows" (Ps. 23:5)? If God is your God, don't you have everything? Who can measure the full capacity of our wishes? But the immeasurable wealth of God exceeds it. Are you not complete when God is yours?

With God you have music fit for heaven, for He is the Maker of heaven. All the music of the sweetest instruments cannot compare to the melody of this sweet promise.

Dwell in the light of the Lord and let your soul be ravished with His love. Live up to your privileges and rejoice with unspeakable joy.

THE PROMISED LAND

Now there is in store for me
the crown of righteousness.
2 Timothy 4:8

Come with me, believer, and let us sit on top of Mount Nebo and view that good land (Deut. 32:48-49). Do you see that little river of death glistening in the sunlight? Across that river, do you see the pinnacles of the eternal city? If you could fly across that city, you would see a sign on each mansion: This is reserved for So-and-so. He will live here forever with God. One of these mansions is your inheritance.

If you believe in the Lord Jesus, if you have repented of sin and have a renewed heart, you are one of the Lord's people. There is a place reserved for you, a crown set aside, a harp ready for you to play.

GOOD SEED

They have no root.
Luke 8:13

If my heart remains unsoftened, unfertilized by grace, the good seed may bloom for a season, but it eventually withers. Is this my case? Have I been putting on a good show on the outside, without any true life on the inside?

Good growth takes place upward and downward at the same time. Am I rooted in sincere faith and love for Jesus? It cannot flourish when the heart is rocky, unbroken, unsanctified.

I don't want a godliness that sprouts up but doesn't last. Let me count the cost of following Jesus. Let me feel the energy of His Holy Spirit. Then I will have a thriving and lasting seed in my soul.

JANUARY 12

BELONGING TO CHRIST

And you are of Christ.
1 Corinthians 3:23

You belong to Christ because you have been bought by His blood. You have been dedicated to His service. Show the world that you are the servant, the friend, the bride of Jesus. When you are tempted to sin, say, "I can't do this sinful thing, because I belong to Christ." It just does not make sense for a friend of Christ to sin.

When the cause of God invites you, give yourself to it. If you have professed faith in Christ, that is your profession. Act like a Christian. Let the way you talk make people think of Christ. Let your conduct conjure up pictures of heaven. Let everyone know, by the way you live, that you belong to the Savior. Let them recognize His love and holiness in you, because you are of Christ.

Ship Wreck

*Now Jehoshaphat built a fleet of trading ships
to go to Ophir for gold, but they never set
sail – they were wrecked at Ezion Geber.*
1 Kings 22:48

May we have the grace to praise God not only for the shiploads of blessings He gives us, but also for the ships broken at Ezion Geber. We should not envy the more successful. Nor should we complain about our losses, as if we were the only ones who suffered misfortunes. Like Jehoshaphat, we may be precious in the Lord's sight, even though our schemes end in disappointment.

Jehoshaphat's experience should serve as a warning to the rest of God's people. We should avoid being "unequally yoked together" with unbelievers (2 Cor. 6:14).

We must love Jesus so much that we remain holy, undefiled, separate from sinners.

MIGHTY TO SAVE

Mighty to save.
Isaiah 63:1

Christ is not only "mighty to save" those who repent, but He is able to make people repent. Yes, He will carry to heaven those who believe. But He shows His might also in giving people new hearts and establishing faith inside them.

Christ does not bring a person to repentance and then let him shift for himself. He who begins the work carries it on (Phil. 1:6). He who puts the first germ of life in the dead soul strengthens it, until it breaks the bonds of sin and the soul leaps from the earth, perfected in glory.

With others, or with you, Jesus is "mighty to save." The best proof lies in the fact that He has already saved you.

GOD'S PROMISES

Do as you promised.
2 Samuel 7:25

God's promises were never meant to be thrown aside like wastepaper. He wants them to be used. Nothing pleases our Lord more than to see His promises put in circulation.

When a Christian grasps a promise, if he does not take it to God, he dishonors him. But when he rushes to the throne of grace and cries, "This is all I have to stand on – Your promise," then his desire is granted.

Don't think that God will be bothered when you keep reminding Him of His promises. Does the sun get tired of shining? Does the fountain get tired of flowing? No. God loves to hear the requests of needy souls. It is His nature to keep His promises. He delights in giving out favors. He is more ready to hear than you are to ask.

CHRIST, OUR HELPER

"I myself will help you," declares the LORD.
Isaiah 41:14

This morning Jesus is speaking to each one of us. "Helping you is the least of the things I can do for you. I have done far more – and I will continue to do more. Before the world began, I chose you. I made a covenant for you. I laid aside My glory and became a man for you. I gave My life for you. And if I did all this, I will surely help you now.

Bring your empty pitcher. This well will fill it. Gather up all your wants and bring them here – your emptiness, your sorrows, your needs. The river of God is flowing: it is ready to supply your needs. You can go forth with this assurance: The Eternal God is your helper."

WITH CHRIST

Then I looked, and there before me
was the Lamb, standing on Mount Zion.
Revelation 14:1

The major object of contemplation in the heavenly city is "the Lamb of God, who takes away the sins of the world" (Jn. 1:29). That's what captured John's attention. Nothing else was as important as that Divine Being, who redeemed us by His blood.

It is a joyous experience to have daily fellowship with Jesus. We will have the same joy in heaven, but to a higher degree. We will enjoy the constant vision of His presence. We will live with Him forever.

To be with Christ is to be in heaven and to be in heaven is to be with Christ. All that you need to be content, to be truly blessed, is to be with Christ.

PERFECT REST

There remains, then, a Sabbath-rest
for the people of God.
Hebrews 4:9

Our situation in heaven will be much different from what it is here. Here we are born to work hard and grow weary. But our days of weariness will not last forever. Here our rest is partial. There, it is perfect. Here, we remain unsettled; we feel there is always so much more to do. There, all are at rest; they rest in the bosom of God Himself.

Think of that, if you are weary from your labors. Think of that eternal rest. Can you even imagine it? It is a rest that "remains."

Here on earth, my best joys are mortal. But there, everything is immortal. The immortal being is totally absorbed in infinite delight.

WITHOUT CHRIST

I looked for him but did not find him.
Song of Songs 3:1

Tell me where you lost track of Christ, and I will tell you where you will probably find Him. Did you lose Him in the prayer closet by neglecting regular prayer? Then that is where you should look for Him. Did you lose Christ when you turned to sin? Then find Him by giving up the sin. Did you lose Christ by neglecting the Scriptures? Then find Him in the Scriptures.

Look for Christ where you lost Him. He has not gone away.

It is dangerous to be without your Lord. Without Christ you are like a sheep without a shepherd, like a tree without water at its roots. Seek Him with your whole heart, and you will find Him.

Give yourself thoroughly to this search, and once again He will be your joy and gladness.

JESUS, THE SHEPHERD-PRIEST

Now Abel kept flocks.
Genesis 4:2

Abel, the shepherd, offered a sacrifice of blood, dedicating it to God. He serves as an early symbol of Jesus. Abel is a shepherd and a priest, since he offers a sweet-smelling sacrifice to God. In him, we see our Lord Jesus, who brings before His Father a pleasing sacrifice.

It is a very precious thing to stand at the altar of our Good Shepherd, to see Him bleeding there as a slaughtered priest, and then to hear His blood speaking peace to His whole flock. He speaks peace to our consciences, peace between God and humanity, peace throughout eternity for blood-washed souls.

CROSSING THE SEA

And so all Israel will be saved.
Romans 11:26

When Moses sang at the Red Sea, it was his joy to know that all Israel was safe. And at the end of time, when all God's chosen ones will sing the song of Moses and of the Lamb, this will be the boast of Jesus – "None has been lost" (Jn. 17:12).

There will be no vacant thrones in heaven. All the ones God has chosen, all those redeemed by Christ, all those the Spirit has called, all who believe in Jesus, will safely cross the dividing sea. We have not all crossed over yet, but we are on the way. The vanguard of our army has already reached the shore. We are marching through the depths. Right now we are following our Leader in to the heart of the sea. Soon the last of the chosen ones will have crossed the sea. Then when all are safe, will the song of triumph be heard.

PRIDE AND GRACE

Son of man, how is the wood of a vine better than that of a branch on any of the trees in the forest?
Ezekiel 15:2

JANUARY 22

These words are for the humbling of God's people. By God's goodness, they have been fruitful, planted in good soil. The Lord strung these vines on the walls of His sanctuary, and they bear fruit for His glory. But what are they without God? What are they without the continual influence of the Spirit making them fruitful?

Get rid of pride, believer. You have no reason for it. The more you have, the more you are in debt to God. Consider where you came from. Where would you be without God's grace? If you amount to anything now, it is because of God's grace. That's what makes you different from anyone else. You may be valiant in the cause of God's truth, but if grace had not grabbed you, you would be just as valiant in unholy causes.

CHRIST'S FOOTSTEPS

I have exalted a young man from among the people.
Psalm 89:19

Christ was "among the people" so that He might know our needs and sympathize with us. In all our sorrows we have His sympathy. Temptation, pain, disappointment, weakness, weariness, poverty – He knows them all, for He has felt them all. Remember this, Christian, and let it comfort you.

However difficult and painful your road may be, it is marked by the footsteps of the Savior. Even when you reach the dark valley of the shadow of death and the deep waters of the surging Jordan, you will find His footprints there.

Wherever you go, He has gone. Each burden we have to carry has at one time been laid on the shoulders of Immanuel.

SAVED FROM THE SNARE

Surely he will save you from the fowler's snare.
Psalm 91:3

God saves His people from the fowler's snare in two ways. First He saves them from the snare by keeping them away from it. But if they should get caught in the snare, He gets them out of it.

How does God save us from the snare? He often uses trouble. God knows that our backsliding leads to our destruction.

In mercy, He sends the rod of affliction. We say, "Why, Lord?" not knowing that our trouble has been God's way of protecting us from a far greater evil. At other times, God saves us from the snare by giving us spiritual strength.

GOD'S KINDNESS

I will tell of the kindnesses of the LORD.
Isaiah 63:7

What kindnesses have you experienced? You may be gloomy now, but are you forgetting that blessed hour when Jesus met you? Have you forgotten these moments of first love? Did you ever have a sickness that He healed? Were you ever in need, and He supplied it? Were you ever in dire straits, and He delivered you? Have you never been helped in times of need? I know you have.

Go back, then, to the choice mercies of yesterday. It may be dark now, but if you light up the lamps of the past, they will glitter through the darkness. They will help you trust in the Lord until the day breaks and the shadows flee.

OUR FATHER

Your heavenly Father.
Matthew 6:26

Father! Oh what a precious word that is! Here is authority. Because He is our Father, we owe Him obedience. Here is affection mingled with authority. The obedience that God's children show Him must be loving obedience. Don't go about God's service as slaves might go about their taskmaster's toil. Enjoy it, because it is your Father's desire. Yield your bodies as instruments of righteousness, because righteousness is what your Father wants.

Father! Here we find honor and love. How great is a father's love for his children! It goes beyond friendship. It goes beyond mere benevolence. If an earthly father watches over his children with constant love and care, how much more does our heavenly Father? Abba, Father!

FULLNESS IN CHRIST

*From the fullness of his grace we have
all received one blessing after another.*
John 1:16

There is fullness in Christ. There is fullness in the justification He offers. There is fullness in His deliverance. There is fullness of victory in His death; there is fullness of power in His resurrection.

There is fullness of blessings of every sort and shape – a fullness of grace to forgive us, to make us new, to make us holy, to keep us safe, to make us more like Christ.

There is fullness for all situations – a fullness of comfort in affliction, of guidance in prosperity. There is fullness of every divine attribute, of wisdom, power, love. Come, believer, get all your need supplied. Ask for much, and you will get much. This fullness is inexhaustible, and it is stored up where all the needy may reach it – in Jesus.

COMPLETE IN HIM

JANUARY 28

Perfect in Christ.
Colossians 1:28

You are not perfect. You know that in your soul. You know your heart too well to even dream for a moment of any perfection in yourself. But in the middle of this sad situation, there is comfort for you – you are "perfect in Christ." In God's sight, you are "complete in Him." Right now, you stand accepted by God.

Yet we have a second perfection, too, that is yet to be realized. We can look forward to the time when every stain of sin will be removed from us.

We will be presented faultless before God's throne, without spot or wrinkle. Then we will know and taste and feel the happiness of this vast but short phrase: "Perfect in Christ."

OUR GOAL

We fix our eyes not on what is seen,
but on what is unseen.
2 Corinthians 4:18

In our Christian pilgrimage, it is good to look forward. Our crown is in front of us, our goal lies ahead. Looking ahead with the eye of faith, we see the hope, joy, comfort, and inspiration of the future. We see sin cast out, the body of sin and death destroyed, the soul made perfect. We see ourselves as partakers of the inheritance of the saints.

Looking even further, the believer's enlightened eyes see the crossing of death's river and the climbing of the hills of light, on which stands the celestial city.

The believer can see himself entering the pearly gates, hailed as a conqueror, crowned by Christ, embraced in the arms of Jesus, glorified with Him, offered a seat on His throne.

JANUARY 30

OPPORTUNE TIME

As soon as you hear the sound of marching
in the tops of the balsam trees, move quickly.
2 Samuel 5:24

There are times when the "sound of marching" is heard in your personal life. You become especially powerful in prayer. The Spirit gives you joy and gladness. The Scripture is open to you, and you apply its promises. You are walking in the light of God's presence. Your dedication to Christ is full and free, and you stay in close communion with Him.

Now is the time to "move quickly." Get rid of some evil habit. Develop new habits of prayer in this time when you feel close to Christ. Learn new ways to be holy now that you are tapping into Christ's power.

EFFECTS OF RIGHTEOUSNESS

The LORD Our Righteousness.
Jeremiah 23:6

Though distress may afflict me, though Satan assaults me, I can rest in the fact that Christ has made me righteous. On the cross He said, "It is finished!" If it is finished, then I am complete in Him, and I can rejoice – "not having a righteousness of my own that comes from the law, but that which is through faith in Christ" (Phil. 3:9).

There is no one holier than those who have received Christ's righteousness. We have had righteousness imputed to our account. That helps us value the righteousness imparted to our lives.

It should give the Christian a sense of calm, a sense of quiet peace, to think about the perfect righteousness of Christ.

FEBRUARY

DAILY PRAISE

May they sing of the ways of the LORD,
for the glory of the LORD is great.
Psalm 138:5

When do Christians begin to sing? When they leave their burden at the foot of the cross. Do you recall the day when your fetters fell off? Do you remember the place when Jesus met you and said, "I have loved you with an everlasting love" (Jer. 31:3)?

But it is not only at the beginning of their Christian lives that people have a reason to sing. As long as they live, Christians keep discovering reasons to sing of the ways of the Lord. Their daily experience makes them say, "I will extol the LORD at all times; His praise will always be on my lips" (Ps. 34:1).

Magnify the Lord today!

Forgiven by the Blood

*Without the shedding of
blood there is no forgiveness.*
Hebrews 9:22

This is an eternal truth. Sin cannot be pardoned without atonement. That means that there is not hope for me outside of Christ, for there is no other blood that can truly take away my sin. All of us are equal in our need of Him. We may be moral, generous, friendly, or patriotic – but there is no exception to the rule.

Sin will yield to nothing less powerful than the blood of the Savior. We should be glad that we have a way to be forgiven. Why go looking for another?

We don't need to "feel" saved. If your conscience troubles you, don't look for "proofs" of your salvation. Look to the cross. See Jesus suffering for you. Trust in His blood for your forgiveness.

A LIVING SACRIFICE

Therefore, brethren, we are debtors.
Romans 8:12 KJV

Christ said, "It is finished!" Whatever His people owed was wiped from the books. Christ has satisfied the divine justice. The account is settled. The bill has been nailed to the cross. The receipt has been given.

But then, because we are not debtors anymore in that sense, we become ten times more God's debtors in another sense. Think about how much you owe to God's sovereignty, to His unmerited love, to His forgiving grace.

You owe God a great deal. You owe yourself and all that you have. So give yourself as a living sacrifice. It is only your reasonable service (Rom. 12:1).

THE LORD'S LOVE

As the LORD loves the Israelites.
Hosea 3:1

Look back through your experience. See how the Lord has led you through the wilderness, how He has fed and clothed you every day, how He has put up with your complaining. Think of how His grace has been sufficient for you in all your troubles, how His blood has pardoned all your sins, and how His rod and staff have comforted you.

After you have looked back on the way the Lord has loved you in the past, let your faith anticipate His future love. The one who has loved and pardoned you will never stop loving and pardoning. Even death cannot separate you from His love.

The more we meditate on the way "the Lord loves the Israelites" – and how He loves us – the more our hearts burn within us. We long to love Him more.

THE FATHER'S LOVE

*The Father has sent his Son
to be the Savior of the world.*
1 John 4:14

Have you put your confidence in Christ Jesus? Have you placed your faith solely in Him? Are you united with Him? Then you are also united with the God of heaven. The "Ancient of Days" is therefore your Father and your friend.

Have you considered the depths of Yahweh's love? Meditate on this today. The Father sent Him! Jesus does what the Father plans.

In the wounds of the dying Savior, see the love of the great I AM. Every time you think of Jesus, think of the eternal loving Father who sent Him.

GOD'S MERCIES

And pray in the Spirit on all occasions.
Ephesians 6:18

Think of all the prayers you have prayed, ever since you first learned how. We have prayed for grace to help us live holy lives, for a fresh assurance of our salvation, for the application of God's promises, for deliverance from temptation, for strength to do God's work, for comfort in times of testing. We are like beggars, regularly approaching God to ask whatever our souls need.

Your soul has not grown rich on its own. It is dependent, relying on God for its daily allowance of blessing. That is why we pray the whole range of spiritual mercies we need.

Our wants have been countless, but God's supplies have been infinite.

Our prayers have been as varied as the mercies are plentiful.

A BETTER COUNTRY

Get up, go away! For this is not your resting place.
Micah 2:10

All of us will hear this message sooner or later. "Get up! It's time to leave your home, your business, your family, and your friends. It is time to take your final journey." We know that there is a dark and stormy river called death. God tells us to cross it, promising to be with us. And what comes then?

We know enough about the heavenly land to rejoice when we are finally summoned there. We will be leaving all we have known and loved here, but we are headed to our Father's house. We will be with Jesus. We will live forever with the Lord we love and with all His people. Christian, meditate on heaven as much as you can; it will help you to press on, to forget how difficult the journey can be. This valley of tears is only the pathway to a better country.

THE NAME OF JESUS

You are to give him the name Jesus.
Matthew 1:21

If there is one name sweeter than any other, it is the name of Jesus. Jesus! It is a name that moves the harps of heaven to make beautiful melody. Jesus! It is woven into the very fabric of our worship.

Many of our hymns begin with it, and hardly any, if they're worth anything, end without mentioning it.

It is the sum total of all delights. It is the music ringing from the bells of heaven, an ocean of things to think about. It gathers up all the hallelujahs of eternity in just five letters.

Jesus!

GOD'S GUIDANCE

So David inquired of the Lord.
2 Samuel 5:23

Learn this from David. Take no step without God. If you want to stay on the right path, let God be your compass. If you want to steer your ship safely through the storm, let God's hand rest on the tiller. We will avoid many rocks, many shoals and quicksands, if we let our Father take the helm.

Another preacher has said, "He that goes on before the cloud of God's providence goes on a fool's errand."

We must let God's providence lead the way. If we run ahead, we'll have to run back again. So let's take all our pressing questions to Him. Ask Him, "What should I do?"

DANGERS OF PROSPERITY

I know how to abound.
Philippians 4:12 KJV

The Christian is more apt to disgrace his faith in prosperity than in adversity. It is a dangerous thing to be prosperous. The material bounty that God gives us often leads us to neglect spiritual things. Our souls grow lean as our bodies grow fat.

Many have asked God's blessings in order to satisfy their own desires. They are full of God's providential mercies, but they lack God's grace, and they have little gratitude for what they have received.

When we are full, we tend to forget God. Rest assured it is harder to know how to be full than it is to know how to be hungry. Because of our pride and forgetfulness, prosperity is difficult for us. So be sure to ask God to teach you how to abound.

IMITATE JESUS

They took note that these men had been with Jesus.
Acts 4:13

A Christian should be a striking likeness of Jesus Christ. The best "life of Christ" is His living biography, written out in the words and actions of His people. Think kindly, speak kindly, and act kindly – so that people will say about you, "He has been with Jesus."

Imitate Jesus in His holiness. He was zealous; you should be, too, always going about doing good. He was self-denying; you should be, too. He was devout; you, too, should be fervent in your prayers. He submitted to His Father's will; and so should you. He was patient; and you, too, must learn to endure. Above all, try to forgive your enemies, as Jesus did. Forgive as you hope to be forgiven. Be God-like in all you do and say, so that everyone who sees you may say, "He has been with Jesus."

SUFFERING AND COMFORT

For just as the sufferings of Christ flow over into our lives, so also through Christ our comfort overflows.
2 Corinthians 1:5

When the night approaches and the storm threatens, the heavenly Captain is especially close to His crew. This is a wonderful thing. Why? For one thing, trials make more room for comfort. Great hearts can only be made by great trials. Then there is more room for grace.

Another reason is this. When we have troubles, we have our closest dealings with God. When the barn is full we think we can live without God. But clean the idols out of the house, and then we must honor the true God.

There is no prayer half so hearty as that which comes up from the depths of the soul, through deep trials and afflictions. So do not fret over your heavy troubles. They are the heralds of great mercies.

ADOPTED

Dear friends, now we are children of God.
1 John 3:2

When we consider the kind of people we were and how corrupt we still feel sometimes, this adoption is truly amazing. We are the children of God! What an honored relationship this is, and what privileges it brings! What care and tenderness the child expects from his father, and what love a father feels toward his child! All of that – and more – we now have through Christ.

How is it with your heart? Does grace seem like a fading spark, trampled underfoot? Does your faith almost fail you? Don't worry. You are not to live by your feelings or even your gracious acts. You must live simply by faith in Christ. Wherever we are, even in the depths of sorrow, the message comes to us: "Now we are children of God." The Holy Spirit will purify our minds. And we will see our Lord as He is.

DAILY GRACE

*Day by day the king gave Jehoiachin
a regular allowance as long as he lived.*
2 Kings 25:30

A daily allowance is all anyone really needs. We don't need tomorrow's supplies. If we have enough for each day, as the days arrive, we will not be in need.

The fact is, that's all we can really enjoy. We cannot eat or drink or wear more than one day's supply of food and clothing. "Enough for the day" is not only as good as a feast – it is all that even the hungriest glutton can enjoy. This is all we should expect. We have a regular allowance from the King Himself; it is enough for the day, and it will last forever.

In matters of grace, you need a daily supply. You cannot store up spiritual strength. Day by day you must seek God's help. Never go hungry while the daily bread of grace is on the table of mercy.

GLORIFYING JESUS

To him be glory both now and forever.
2 Peter 3:18

Believer, you are eagerly anticipating the time when you will join the saints in giving eternal glory to Jesus. But are you glorifying Him now? Why not make this your prayer today?

"Lord, help me to glorify You. I am poor, but help me to glorify You by being content. I am sick, but help me to honor You with my patience. I have talents; help me to use them for You. I have time, Lord; help me to redeem it so that I can serve You. I have a heart that feels things deeply, Lord; let my heart glow with a flame of passion for You. I have a head that thinks, Lord; fill it with thoughts of You and that please You.

You have put me in the world for something, Lord. Show me what that is. I am Yours. Take me, and show me how to glorify You now."

LEARNING CONTENTMENT

I am not saying this because I am in need, for I have learned to be content whatever the circumstances.
Philippians 4:11

Contentment is not a natural propensity of man. Covetousness, discontent, and complaining are as natural to us as weeds are to soil. But the precious things of the earth must be cultivated. If we want flowers, we must garden. Now contentment is one of the flowers of heaven. It will not grow naturally. Only the new nature can produce it, and even then we must take special care of the grace God has planted inside us.

Paul says, "I have learned to be content." Do not indulge the notion that you can be content without learning. And you can't learn without discipline.

So my brother or sister, hold back your next complaint, however natural it may be, and continue as a diligent pupil in the College of Contentment.

THE WELL OF GOD

Isaac lived near Beer Lahai Roi.
Genesis 25:11

The name means "the well of the Living One who sees me." Isaac lived there. He made the well of the living and all-seeing God the source of his livelihood. This is the true test of a person – where does his soul live? Best of all, here he enjoyed fellowship with the living God.

We should learn to live in the presence of the living God. He should be a well for us – delightful, comforting, unfailing, springing up to eternal life (Jn. 4:14). The well of the Creator never fails to nourish us.

The Lord has shown Himself to be a true helper. His name is Shaddai, the all-sufficient God. So let us live in close fellowship with Him, drawing daily from His well.

GROWTH THROUGH TRIALS

Tell me what charges you have against me.
Job 10:2

Are you being tested like Job? Perhaps the Lord is trying to develop some aspects of your character – faith, love, and hope. Some of these might never be discovered if it weren't for trials. Hard times are often the dark background against which God sets the jewels of His children's faith, hope, and love – they shine all the brighter.

Count on this: God often sends us trials to help us discover new attributes of our Christianity and not only to discover them, but to grow in them.

God often takes away our comforts and privileges in order to make us better Christians. Well, Christian, does this help explain your troubles? Isn't God helping you to grow?

BLESSINGS THROUGH PRAYER

*Once again I will yield to the plea of
the house of Israel and do this for them.*
Ezekiel 36:37

Prayer is the forerunner of mercy. Search through sacred history, and you will find that hardly ever did a great mercy come to this world without prayer paving its way. God has given many blessings without being asked, but still, great prayer has always preceded great mercy.

As you think about the great joys of your life, you have seen them as answers to prayer. Prayer is always the preface to blessing. So we see the value of prayer. If we had the blessings without asking for them, we would take them for granted. But prayer makes our mercies more precious than diamonds. The things we ask for are precious, but we do not realize how precious until we have earnestly asked God for them.

COMFORT FROM GOD

God, who comforts the downcast.
2 Corinthians 7:6

Who can comfort us like God? One word from God is like a piece of gold, and the Christian is like the goldsmith, who hammers out the promise for weeks on end. So then, Christian, you don't need to sit down in despair. Go to the Comforter. Ask Him to give you consolation.

You are a poor, dry well. So Christian, when you are dry, go to God. Ask Him to dowse your soul with joy. Then your joy will be full.

Don't go to earthly friends. But go first and foremost to the God who comforts the downcast, and you will soon find yourself saying, "When anxiety was great within me, your consolation brought joy to my soul" (Ps. 94:19).

GOD'S PROMISES

God has said.
Hebrews 13:5

When we hide ourselves within the fortress of this statement, all the distresses of life, all its traps and trials seem light and easy to bear. This simple truth gives us delight in times of quiet meditation, and it gives us strength for our daily battles.

There may be a promise in God's Word that would fit your situation exactly, but you may not know it, so you miss out on its comfort. You are like a prisoner in a dungeon, with a ring of keys. One of the keys would unlock the door and free you. But if you don't look for it, you will remain a prisoner, though your liberty is so close at hand. "He has said" is the source of all wisdom.

Let it dwell in you richly.

COVENANT OF STRENGTH

But his bow remained steady,
his strong arms stayed limber, because
of the hand of the Mighty One of Jacob.
Genesis 49:24

Why did Joseph resist temptation? God helped him. We can do nothing without God's power. All true strength comes from "the Mighty One of Jacob." The strength God gives is covenant strength. We Christians love to think of God's covenant.

If there were no covenant, we would have no hope, for all God's grace proceeds from it, as light and heat from the sun. No angels ascend or descend except on that ladder that Jacob saw – and at the top of that ladder was God, making a covenant with Him.

Dear Christian, you may have been wounded by enemy archers, but your bow is still strong. Be sure to give all the glory to "the Mighty One of Jacob."

PROMISE OF GOD'S PRESENCE

Never will I leave you.
Hebrews 13:5

Be bold to believe because God has said, "Never will I leave you, never will I forsake you." In this promise, God gives His people everything. Suddenly all the attributes of God are there for our use. Is He mighty? He shows His strength on behalf of those who trust Him. Is He love? Then He lovingly shows us His mercy.

Anything you could want, anything you could ask for, anything you could ever need in time or eternity – this text contains it all.

Everything living or dying, in this world or the next, now and on the resurrection morning – it is all here for you.

ABUNDANCE OF GRACE

I will bless them and the places surrounding
my hill. I will send down showers in season;
there will be showers of blessing.
Ezekiel 34:26

Only God can send showers upon the vegetation of earth. Grace is like that, too. It is a gift of God; we cannot create it ourselves.

God's grace is also plentiful. He sends showers, and so it is with grace. If God gives a blessing, He usually gives it in such proportions that we don't have room to receive it all. Grace to make us zealous, to get us through this life and on to heaven.

God's grace, like rain, is also seasonable. What is your season this morning? Are you in a drought? Then that is the season for God's showers. Is it a season of weariness and dark clouds? Then that is the time for God's blessing.

SHELTER FROM THE STORM

The coming wrath.
Matthew 3:7

Sinner, this is your present situation. No hot drops have yet fallen, but a shower of fire is coming. No terrible winds howl around you, but God's hurricane is gathering up its awesome artillery. The floodgates are still dammed up by God's mercy, but soon they shall open. Then where will you flee?

God's hand of mercy is now outstretched, offering to lead you to Christ. He will shelter you from the storm. You know you need Him. Believe in Him, throw yourself upon His mercy, and let the approaching storm of God's wrath blow over you.

REMAIN IN JESUS

Salvation comes from the LORD.
Jonah 2:9

Salvation is the work of God. Only He can bring life to the soul that is "dead in … transgressions and sins" (Eph. 2:1). Only He can maintain the soul in its spiritual life.

If I have faith or hope or love, they are God's gifts to me. If my life is steady and consistent, that's because God upholds me with His hand. I can do nothing to preserve myself, except what God does first inside of me.

Whatever I have, all my goodness comes from God. Without Jesus I can do nothing. As a branch cannot bear fruit unless it remains in the vine (Jn. 15:4), neither can I, unless I remain in Jesus.

Safe with God

*If you make the Most High your dwelling –
even the Lord, who is my refuge.*
Psalm 91:9

The Christian knows no change when it comes to God. He may be rich today and poor tomorrow. He may be sick today and well tomorrow. He may be happy today and distressed tomorrow. But there is no change in where he stands with God.

If God loved me yesterday, He loves me today. Let all my prospects fall through; let my hopes be blasted; let my joy wither – I will never lose what I have in God. He is my safe dwelling place.

I am a pilgrim in this world, but at home with God. On the earth I wander, but in God I live in peace.

HOPE – PRESENT AND FUTURE

My hope comes from Him.
Psalm 62:5

If we are looking for any satisfaction from this world, our hopes will be dashed. But if we look to God to supply our wants, both temporal and spiritual, we will be satisfied. We may always draw from the bank of faith and have our needs supplied out of the riches of God's loving-kindness. My Lord never fails to honor His promises. When we bring them to His throne, He never sends them back unanswered.

But we also have hopes beyond this life. We hope soon to be among the multitudes of shining ones before the throne. We look forward to and long for the time when we will be like our glorious Lord.

If these are your hopes, my friend, then live for God. Live with the desire to glorify Him. Only through His grace do you have hope of a future glory.

LAW AND LOVE

I have drawn you with loving-kindness.
Jeremiah 31:3

God uses the thunders of the law and the terrors of judgment to bring us to Christ. But He wins His final victory with loving-kindness. The Prodigal Son set out for his father's house with a great sense of need. But his father saw him a long way off and ran to meet him. That boy took the last few steps toward his father's house with a kiss still warm on his cheek and the welcome music ringing in his ears (Lk. 15). In every case, loving-kindness wins the day.

What Moses could never do with his tablets of stone, Christ does with His wounded hand. May He continue to draw me with His love, until I finally sit down at the wedding feast of the Lamb.

MARCH

WINDS OF AFFLICTION

*Awake, north wind, and come, south wind! Blow on
my garden, that its fragrance may spread abroad.*
Song of Songs 4:16

Anything is better than the dead calm of
indifference. It would be better to call forth the
north wind of trouble if that could somehow be
sanctified to carry the fragrance of our spiritual
growth. Unless it can be said that "the LORD was
not in the wind" (1 Kgs. 19:11), we will not shy
away from even the most wintry blast. We can
honestly welcome any trial, if that will help to
please our Immanuel.

Those Christian virtues that we do not exercise
are like the fragrant nectar that stays slumbering
in the cups of the flowers.

Yet when our wise Gardener allows the winds
of both affliction and comfort to blow on us, these
winds catch our aromas of faith, love, patience,
hope, resignation, joy, and so on, spreading them
far and wide.

SHARPENING OUR WEAPONS

*So all Israel went down to the Philistines to have their
plowshares, mattocks, axes and sickles sharpened.*
1 Samuel 13:20

We are engaged in a great war and we must use
every weapon within our reach. Preaching,
teaching, praying, giving, all must be brought
into action. But most of our tools need sharpen-
ing. We need quickness of perception, tact,
energy, promptness – we must adapt everything
for the Lord's work. We could learn a thing or
two from our enemies. In so doing, we make the
"Philistines" sharpen our weapons.

Various false religions use great energy in
spreading their views. The devils are united in
their rebellion while we believers are divided
as we try to serve Jesus. We should learn from
our enemies how to bless, and not curse, and
how to truly serve our true Lord.

IN FIERY TRIALS

I have chosen thee in the furnace of affliction.
Isaiah 48:10 KJV

Comfort yourself with this thought. Let affliction come – God has chosen me. Whatever may happen to me in this valley of tears, I know that He has chosen me.

Remember this: You have the Son of Man with you in the furnace. You can't see Him, but you can feel the pressure of His hands. Don't be afraid, Christian. Jesus is with you. In all your fiery trials, His presence is both your comfort and safety. He will never leave one whom He has chosen as His own.

So take hold of Him and follow where He leads. Even in the valley of the shadow of death He says, "So do not fear, for I am with you; do not be dismayed, for I am your God" (Is. 41:10).

ALL-SUFFICIENT GRACE

My grace is sufficient for you.
2 Corinthians 12:9

God's chosen ones bear up under every discouragement. They know that all things work together for good, that out of this apparent evil will ultimately arise something good. If we never had to face storms, we would never know how strong the Spirit has made us. The masterworks of God are those people who stand firm in the midst of difficulties.

He who wants to glorify God can count on facing many trials. No one can truly shine for Christ without enduring many conflicts. So if you have a difficult path, rejoice in it. You are demonstrating the all-sufficient grace of God. The God who has been sufficient until now should be trusted to the end.

WATCH AND PRAY

Let us not be like others, who are asleep.
1 Thessalonians 5:6

Christians who isolate themselves and walk alone are liable to grow drowsy. Join with other Christians, though, and you will stay awake, refreshed, encouraged, and will make quicker progress on the road to heaven.

But as you converse with other believers, make sure that your theme is Jesus. Let the eye of faith always be looking to Him. Let your heart be full of Him. Let your lips speak of His worth.

My friend, live close to the cross, and you will not sleep. You are headed toward heaven! That thought alone should keep you alert.

So continue to "watch and pray" (Mt. 26:41), in fellowship with other Christians, so that you don't enter into temptation.

NEW LIFE

You must be born again.
John 3:7

Regeneration is the very basis of salvation. This great work of salvation is supernatural. A person cannot do this by himself. God infuses a whole new principle in a person's heart, renewing the soul, affecting one's entire life. It is not a change of my name, but a renewal of my nature. I am not the man I used to be, but a new man in Christ Jesus.

If you have been born again, your prayer is this: "Lord Jesus, everlasting Father, you are my spiritual parent. If your Spirit had not breathed into me the breath of a new, holy, and spiritual life, I would still be 'dead in transgressions and sins.' My spiritual life is totally derived from You, and I owe it all to You. My life is hidden with Christ in God. It is no longer I who live, but Christ living in me."

FAITH AND JOY

Have faith in God.
Mark 11:22

Faith gives feet to the soul. With faith, the soul can march along the road of God's commandments. Faith is the oil that enables the wheels of holy devotion and earnest piety to move well. Without faith, the wheels grind to a halt.

With faith, I can do everything. Without faith, I have neither the inclination nor the power to do anything to serve God. A little faith is enough to save you, but not enough to do great things for God.

The person of great faith boldly steps forward. She is willing to venture through any difficulty, to get closer to her Lord. The person of great faith fords the raging streams, knowing that God is there, too. That brings joy in even the most trying circumstances.

TRIBULATIONS AND TRIALS

*We must go through many hardships
to enter the kingdom of God.*
Acts 14:22

God's people have their trials. God never intended for His chosen people to be exempt from difficulties. He never promised that they would only experience worldly peace and earthly joy. He never said they would have utter freedom from sickness and the pains of mortality.

But although tribulation is the path of God's children, they have the comfort of knowing that their Master has walked this path first. They have His presence and sympathy to cheer them, His grace to support them, and His example to guide them. And when they reach His kingdom, it will be worth it all.

THE LOVELINESS OF JESUS

He is altogether lovely.
Song of Songs 5:16

The superlative beauty of Jesus is all-attracting. It is not so much to be admired as to be loved. He is more than pleasant, more than fair – He is lovely. This golden word is especially appropriate, because Jesus is the object of our warmest love, a love founded on His intrinsic excellence, the complete perfection of His charms.

We want to imitate His whole life. We want to duplicate His whole character. Even the best of saints have had a few stains on their garments or wrinkles on their brows – but our Lord is nothing but loveliness.

As much as we may love any earthly thing, we cannot love every part of it. But Christ Jesus is the purest gold, light without darkness, bright glory unclouded. He is altogether lovely.

INTOXICATED WITH PLEASURE

When I felt secure, I said, "I will never be shaken."
Psalm 30:6

Let a person march through this world with braced nerve and a brilliant eye, living happily. What will happen? Immobility. When the way is rough, thank God for it.

If God always rocked us in the cradle of prosperity, if we were always dandled on the knees of fortune, if there were never clouds in the sky, if there were never any bitter drops in the wine of this life, we would become intoxicated with pleasure.

Let us bless God, then, for our afflictions. Let us thank Him for our changes. If He did not chasten us like this, we would feel too secure. Continued worldly prosperity is a fiery trial.

THE NATURE OF SIN

So that sin might become utterly sinful.
Romans 7:13

Beware of light thoughts of sin. It is sadly true that even a Christian may grow callous by degrees, so that the same sin that once startled him does not alarm him in the least. So we throw a cloak over sin. We call it by dainty names. Christian, beware of this. By thinking lightly of sin, you may be falling little by little.

How can sin be a little thing? It may seem little but it is capable of great destruction. This "little" thing circled our Savior's head with thorns; it made Him suffer anguish.

If you could weigh even the smallest sin on the scales of eternity, you would run from it as from a serpent. Look on all sin as that which crucified the Savior, and you, too, will see that it is "utterly sinful."

TOUGH LOVE

Love your neighbor.
Matthew 5:43

Perhaps you are saying, "I'd like to love my neighbors, but whenever I do anything, they return ingratitude and contempt." Well, that gives you more opportunity for the heroism of love. Love is no feather bed; it's a battle. The one who dares the most will win the most. If the path of love is rough, tread it boldly.

Love your neighbors through thick and thin. Heap "coals of fire" on their heads (Rom. 12:20), and if they're hard to please, then just try to please your Master.

Even if they spurn your love, your Master does not spurn it. Love your neighbor, for in that way you are following the footsteps of Christ.

TURN TO JESUS

Why stay here until we die?
2 Kings 7:3

This book is mainly intended to strengthen believers, but if you are still unsaved, my heart yearns for you.

Of those who refuse to look to Jesus for salvation, no one escapes final damnation.

The fact is, without His mercy, you have no hope at all. If you seek the Lord, you will find Him. Jesus turns away no one who comes to Him. You will not perish if you trust Him.

I pray that the Holy Spirit will embolden you to get up and go to Jesus. It will not be in vain. When you yourself are saved, broadcast the good news to others. Don't hold back. May the Lord save you before the sun goes down today.

THE STRENGTH OF GRACE

So, if you think you are standing firm,
be careful that you don't fall!
1 Corinthians 10:12

It is a curious fact that there is such a thing as being proud of grace. Someone may say, "I have great faith. I will never fall." But he who boasts of his grace has little grace to boast of. It makes no sense to glory in your own faith and love. Let your confidence be in Christ and His strength. Only He can keep you from falling.

Spend more time in prayer. Take time to adore Him. Read the Scriptures more often – and more earnestly. Watch your life carefully; live closer to God. Let your lifestyle reflect heavenly patterns. Live in a way that makes people sit up and take notice of the fact that you have been with Jesus.

DAILY RICHES

Be strong in the grace that is in Christ Jesus.
2 Timothy 2:1

Within Himself, Christ has grace beyond measure. But He does not keep it to Himself. As a reservoir empties itself into pipes, so Christ has emptied out His grace for His people. Grace, whether its work is to pardon, to cleanse, to preserve, to strengthen, to enlighten, to bring to life, or to restore – grace is always available from Him freely and without price.

Day by day we receive grace from Jesus. As we learn to recognize that this grace comes from Him, we will sense our communion with Him and enjoy this fellowship all the more.

Let us use these daily riches of grace. Let us keep coming back to Him to supply all we need. He is there to provide grace to us.

A STRANGER IN THIS WORLD

I dwell with you as an alien, a stranger.
Psalm 39:12

I may be a stranger, but I am still dwelling with You, Lord. I am naturally alienated from You, but Your grace has brought me close to You. Now, in fellowship with You, I walk through this sinful world as a pilgrim in a foreign country. You are a stranger in Your own world, Lord. People forget You, dishonor You, set up new laws and strange customs, and do not recognize You.

Lord, I don't want to be a citizen in a world where Jesus was a stranger. His pierced hands have loosened the cords that used to bind my soul to this earth.

Now I, too, am a stranger here. But here is the good part: I am a stranger dwelling with You. And You are great company.

PRACTICAL LOVE

Remember the poor.
Galatians 2:10

Why does God allow so many of His children to be poor? There are many reasons. For one, He wants to give those of us who have enough an opportunity to show our love for Jesus. He wants us to show our love not only in our words, but also by our actions.

If we truly love Christ, we will care for those whom He loves. Those who are dear to Him will be dear to us. We should not look on this as a duty but as a great privilege. Remember Jesus' words, "Whatever you did for one of the least of these brothers of mine, you did for me" (Mt. 25:40). Surely this is a strong enough motive to make us want to help others with a willing hand and a loving heart.

Everything we do for God's needy people is accepted by Christ as a gift for Himself.

SPIRIT OF ADOPTION

You are all sons of God through faith in Christ Jesus.
Galatians 3:26

You are as much a child of God as the person with great faith. Peter and Paul, those highly favored apostles, were members of God's family – and so are you. One may have more faith or love than another, but God, our heavenly Father, has the same tender heart toward all. This thought should comfort us as we come to God in prayer, saying, "Our Father."

Yet, while this may comfort us, let us not rest contented with weak faith. If you want to live for Christ's glory and be happy in His service, seek to be filled with the spirit of adoption more and more completely, until perfect love drives away all fear.

WITH FAITH

Strengthened in his faith.
Romans 4:20

Christian, take good care of your faith. Prayer cannot draw down answers from God's throne, unless it is the earnest prayer of one who believes. If I am in trouble, faith helps me find help. Faith is the road on which we travel. Without faith, the road is blockaded.

Faith links me with God. Faith clothes me with His power.

Faith puts the divine power at my disposal.

Faith calls every attribute of God to my defense. It helps me defeat the hosts of hell.

With faith, I march in triumph over my enemies. But without faith, how can I receive anything from the Lord?

CHRIST'S LOVE

My beloved!
Song of Songs 2:8 KJV

We often speak of Christ as our souls' beloved. He is very precious to us, "outstanding among ten thousand ... altogether lovely" (Song 5:10, 16).

The love between Jesus and the church is so strong that the apostle dares to defy the whole universe to separate her from Christ's love. Persecutions cannot do this. Neither can trouble nor hardship nor famine nor danger. "No," he boasts, "in all these things we are more than conquerors through him who loved us" (Rom. 8:35, 37).

O precious Lord, we long to know more of You.

THE SUFFERING SAVIOR

You will be scattered, each to his own home.
You will leave me all alone.
John 16:32

Few knew the sorrows of Gethsemane. Most of Jesus' followers were not sufficiently advanced in grace to be allowed to witness the mysteries of Christ's agony. Only Peter, James, and John could approach the veil of our Lord's mysterious sorrow. Even these could not intrude within the veil. They were left a stone's throw away. Jesus had to go through this experience alone.

Some selected souls, for their own strengthening and that of others, are allowed to enter the inner circle and hear the pleadings of the suffering High Priest. But even these cannot penetrate the secret places of the Savior's grief. There Jesus is "left alone."

Isaac Watts is right when he sings, "All the unknown joys He gives, were bought with agonies unknown."

THE PRAYER OF JESUS

*Going a little farther, he fell
with his face to the ground and prayed.*
Matthew 26:39

There are several instructive features in our Savior's prayer during His time of trial. First, it was a lonely prayer. Believer, you too should withdraw into solitary prayer, especially in times of trial. It was humble prayer. Humility gives us a good foothold in prayer. There is no hope of finding favor with God unless we humble ourselves.

It was filial prayer. He was praying as a Son to His Father. And we too can claim adoption as God's children in our times of trial. It was also persevering prayer. Do not stop until you prevail. Keep praying and keep thanking God for what He provides. It was also a prayer of resignation. Yield to God, and He yields to you. Let God do His will, and He will do what is best for you.

CHRIST'S VOLUNTARY SACRIFICE

*His sweat was like drops
of blood falling to the ground.*
Luke 22:44

The mental pressure arising from our Lord's struggle with temptation forced Him into such a state that His pores exuded great drops of blood. This shows how great the weight of sin must have been. It was already crushing our Lord.

It also shows the mighty power of His love. So we also see the voluntary nature of Christ's sufferings. The blood flowed freely without any wounds inflicted.

He is so oblivious to Himself that His agony drives His blood outward. Instead of rushing inside to nourish His own heart, His blood pushes outward to nourish the hearts of others. This shows us the fullness of the sacrifice He made for us.

FEAR THE LORD

He was heard because of his reverent submission.
Hebrews 5:7

This "reverent submission" is what the Bible often calls "the fear of the Lord." It is a healthy fear that leads to obedience.

But imagine the fears that Satan must have used to attack our Lord, fears that would have led Him away from obedience, had He heeded them.

Jesus had a choice as He prayed in the garden: fear the Lord and yield in obedience to Him or fear everything else that Satan might throw at Him. He chose to fear the Lord, in reverent submission. So should we.

THE KISS OF JUDAS

*"Judas, are you betraying
the Son of Man with a kiss?"*
Luke 22:48

Be on guard when the world puts on a loving face. Whenever someone is about to stab religion, he usually professes great reverence for it. Beware of the sleek-faced hypocrisy that brings heresy right behind it.

But what if I am guilty of the same sin as Judas? Do I live in the world as carelessly as others do and yet profess to follow Jesus? Then I am exposing my religion to ridicule and leading people to disparage the holy name I claim. In that case, I am a Judas.

O Lord, keep me clear in this matter. Make me sincere and true. Never let me betray my Savior.

THE SUBSTITUTE

If you are looking for me, then let these men go.
John 18:8

See how much care Jesus showed for His disciples even in His hour of trial. Jesus surrenders Himself to the enemy but speaks forcefully to set His friends free. For Himself, "as a sheep before her shearers is silent, so he did not open his mouth" (Is. 53:7).

But for His disciples' sake He speaks with Almighty energy. Here is love – constant, self-forgetting, faithful love. Don't we have the very soul of atonement in these words? The Good Shepherd, "lays down his life for the sheep" (Jn. 10:11) and pleads that they must go free. The payment has been made for them. Justice demands that the ones in whose place He stands as a substitute should be "let go."

BECOMING BRAVE

Then all the disciples deserted him and fled.
Matthew 26:56

He never deserted them. But they, fearing for their lives, fled from Him as His sufferings just began. This is just one example of how frail we believers are on our own. At best, we are sheep – and we run off when the wolf comes.

Yet God's grace can make the coward brave. These same apostles who ran like scared rabbits grew to be bold as lions once the Spirit had come upon them.

And the same Spirit can make my timid spirit brave enough to confess my allegiance to the Lord. What anguish must have filled Jesus' heart as He saw His friends run off! O Spirit, keep me from forsaking my beloved Savior.

DEPTHS OF LOVE

This love that surpasses knowledge.
Ephesians 3:19

The love of Christ goes beyond human comprehension. Where can we find the words to describe its sweetness, greatness, and faithfulness?

To begin to get an idea of Jesus' love, we must understand the glory He came from – and how far He came to pour Himself out in shame upon the earth. But who can tell how great His majesty was? He reigned supreme over all creatures, God over all, blessed forever.

And who can tell how low He descended? To bleed, to die, to suffer – these were unthinkable for the very Son of God. To suffer such unparalleled agony, to endure a death of shame and desertion by His Father – this is a depth of love our minds cannot begin to grasp. Let this love fill your heart with adoring gratitude.

GLORY IN SUFFERING

Although he was a son, he learned
obedience from what he suffered.
Hebrews 5:8

The Captain of our salvation was "made perfect" through suffering. Our master's experience teaches us that suffering is necessary.

The true-born child of God should not try to escape it – even if he could. But there is one very comforting thought in the fact of Christ's being "made perfect through suffering." He can sympathize fully with us. We can draw a sustaining power from Christ's sympathy.

Believer, grab onto this thought in your times of agony. Let the thought of Jesus strengthen you as you follow in His steps. Find a sweet support in His sympathy. To suffer for Christ is glory.

TRANSFERS

He was numbered with the transgressors.
Isaiah 53:12

Why did Jesus allow Himself to be counted among sinners? There were many reasons. First, by doing so, He could better serve as their advocate. Our Lord Jesus was also numbered with the transgressors so that their hearts might be drawn toward Him. Wasn't Jesus also listed on the roll of sinners that we might be listed in the roll of saints?

He was holy and was recorded as being holy. We were guilty and listed as guilty. He transfers His name from that list to ours and our names are taken from the guilty roll and added to the roll of acceptance. Jesus has taken our situation upon Himself, and all that Jesus possesses is now ours. His righteousness, His blood – this is our dowry.

HEALED BY HIS LOVE

By his wounds we are healed.
Isaiah 53:5

Pilate handed Jesus over to his soldiers to be scourged. The Roman scourge was a very dreadful instrument of torture. Every time the lash came down on a victim's back, it cut into the flesh and tore it away. Our Savior was, no doubt, tied to a column and beaten this way. We may weep as we imagine the blows upon His precious body.

Jesus stands before you, believer, as a mirror of agonizing love. Can you look at Him without tears?

Feel the healing that His wounds have brought to your life – doesn't your heart melt with love and grief? If we have ever loved our Lord Jesus, that love must be growing now as we consider His agony – the pain He went through for us. It is our sin that has cost Him so much.

APRIL

THE LOVE OF CHRIST

Let him kiss me with the kisses of his mouth.
Song of Songs 1:2

Let us stir some of our own passion for the Lord by looking at this love song between Christ and His church. The "kisses" we receive are the various manifestations of Christ's love for us. The kiss of reconciliation came at our conversion. The kiss of acceptance is still warm on our brow, since we know that God accepts us through His grace. The kiss of ongoing communion with Him is one we long for each day. We walk by faith but we rest in Christ's fellowship. Faith is the road but communion with Jesus is the well from which we drink.

O lover of our souls, come close to us. Let the lips of Your blessing meet the lips of our asking. Let the lips of Your fullness touch the lips of our need.

SILENT WISDOM

But Jesus made no reply, not even to a single charge.
Matthew 27:14

Jesus had never been slow to speak when He was blessing others, but here He does not say a word in His own defense. This silence shows us the nature of his perfect self-sacrifice. His silence also depicts the defenselessness of sin. Nothing can be said to excuse human guilt. By His silence, Jesus also demonstrated the best reply to a hostile world. Calm endurance answers some questions far more conclusively than the loftiest eloquence.

The silent Lamb of God also gave us a grand example of wisdom. The ambiguous and false, the unworthy and mean, will eventually confute themselves. So the truth can afford to be quiet. By His quiet, Jesus conclusively proved Himself to be the true Lamb of God. Be with us, Jesus, and in the silence of our hearts, let us hear the voice of Your love.

THE SCAPEGOAT

So the soldiers took charge of Jesus.
John 19:16

He had been in agony all night. He had been hurried from Caiaphas to Pilate, from Pilate to Herod, and from Herod back again to Pilate. He had little strength left. They were eager for His blood and therefore led Him out to die, weighed down with the cross.

It is Jesus who is brought before the priests and rulers and pronounced guilty. Bearing our sin, in the form of that cross, our great Scapegoat is led away by appointed officers of justice. Is that your sin He is carrying with Him? Have you confessed your sin and trusted in Him? If so, then your sin has been transferred to Christ. Don't let this picture vanish until you have rejoiced in your own deliverance and adored the loving Redeemer who took your sins upon Himself.

RIGHTEOUS IN CHRIST

God made him who had no sin to be
sin for us, so that in him we might
become the righteousness of God.
2 Corinthians 5:21

Do you feel guilty about your sinfulness? Look to your perfect Lord and remember: you are complete in Him. The Lord our Righteousness has put a divine garment on you, so that you may have more than mere human righteousness. You have the righteousness of God!

You know that someday you will stand before God's throne and He will declare you righteous through Christ.

But you are accepted just as thoroughly today, even with all your sinfulness. Grab on to this thought: You are perfect in Christ. Wearing His garment you are as holy as the Holy One.

CARRYING THE CROSS

They seized Simon from Cyrene, and put the cross on him and made him carry it behind Jesus.
Luke 23:26

Note that Jesus did not suffer to keep you from suffering. He bears the cross not for you to escape it, but for you to endure it. But we can comfort ourselves with this thought: As with Simon, it is not our cross, but Christ's cross that we carry. When you are mocked for your devotion to Jesus, remember it is *His* cross. The mark of His blood-red shoulder is on the very wood. He goes before you. Take up that cross daily and follow Him.

One more thing: Simon carried the cross for a short time, but it gave him lasting honor. In the same way, we carry the cross for a little while at most, but then we will receive a crown of glory.

HIGHWAY OF HOLINESS

Let us, then, go to him outside the camp.
Hebrews 13:13

Christ was "not of the world." His life and teaching were a constant protest against conformity with the world. He had unmatchable affection for humanity, but He was still separate from sinners. In the same way, Christ's people must "go to Him outside the camp." We must be prepared to tread the straight and narrow path.

We must have bold, unflinching, lionlike hearts, loving Christ and His truth far more than we love the world.

You cannot grow very much in grace while you are conformed to the world. The life of separation may be a path of sorrow, but it is the highway of safety. The highway of holiness is the highway of communion with Christ.

DISHONOR

*How long, O men, will you
turn my glory into shame?*
Psalm 4:2

One writer had noted the mocking "honors" that
the blinded people gave to Jesus, their King.

1. They gave Him a procession of honor. This
   is the ovation they gave the One who came
   to overthrow humanity's foes – derisive
   shouts and cruel taunts instead of paeans
   of praise.
2. They gave Him the wine of honor. They offered
   the criminal's numbing death drink.
3. He was provided with a guard of honor, who
   gambled over His garments.
4. A throne of honor was found for Him on the
   bloody tree. The cross was the full expression
   of the world's feeling toward Him.
   In each case, men turned Jesus' glory into
   shame.

SUFFERING SINNERS

For if men do these things when the tree
is green, what will happen when it is dry?
Luke 23:31

There are many interpretations for this intriguing question. Here is a good one. "If I, the innocent substitute for sinners, suffer like this, what will happen when the sinner himself – the dry tree – falls into the hands of an angry God?"

You rich, high-living, self-righteous sinners – what kind of life will you have when God finally judges you? We cannot sum up in one word all the sorrows that came upon Jesus, who died for us.

So it is impossible to say what streams, what oceans of grief must come upon your soul if you die without Christ. By the agonies of Christ, by His wounds, and by His blood, do not bring on yourselves God's wrath. Trust in the Son of God, and you will never die.

GRATITUDE AND GRIEF

*A large number of people followed him,
including women who mourned and wailed for him.*
Luke 23:27

Amid the contentious crowd that hounded the redeemer to His doom, there were some gracious souls who vented their anguish with wailing and lamentation. Those women had their reasons to love Christ and weep, but so do I. Perhaps one was the widow of Nain, who saw her son brought back to life. But I have also been raised to newness of life.

Perhaps another was Peter's mother-in-law, cured of a fever. But I have been cured of a greater disease: sin itself. Surely Mary Magdalene was there, from whom Christ had cast seven devils. But He cast a whole legion of evil out of me. So since I owe as much to my Savior as these women did, let me join them in gratitude and grief.

CALVARY'S COMFORT

The place, which is called Calvary.
Luke 23:33 KJV

Calvary is the hill of our comfort. The house of our consolation is built with the wood of the cross. The temple of heavenly blessing is founded on that riven rock – riven by the spear that pierced His side. No scene in sacred history gladdens the soul like Calvary's tragedy.

Light springs from the midday midnight of Golgotha, and every herb of the field blooms sweetly beneath the shadow of the once-cursed tree. The bitter herbs of Gethsemane have taken away the bitter taste of life.

So Calvary's comfort is rare and rich. We would never have known Christ's love in all its heights and depths if He had not died. If you want to know love, come to Calvary, and see the Man of Sorrows die.

FROM SUFFERING TO GLORY

I am poured out like water,
and all my bones are out of joint.
Psalm 22:14

In soul and body, our Lord felt Himself to be weak as water poured on the ground. When the cross was placed in its socket, He was shaken violently, His ligaments strained, nerves pained, bones dislocated. In His own consciousness, overpowered by faintness, He must have become nothing but a mass of misery. He drained His cup of sorrow and tasted every drop.

As we kneel before the throne of our ascended Savior, let us drink of the cup of His strength so that we may be ready for our time of trial. Every part of His body suffered, but He came through it all, into His power and glory. Even so shall His spiritual body, the church, come through the furnace with not so much as the smell of fire upon it.

COMMUNION AT THE CROSS

My heart has turned to wax;
it has melted away within me.
Psalm 22:14

Imagine how the suffering Savior longed for God to be close to Him, for this is the time a man needs God the most – when his heart is melting within him. Believer, come to the cross and humbly adore the King of Glory. Realize that He was once brought far lower, in mental distress and inward anguish, than any of us.

If you feel far away from God, if you lack a sense of His love, then – especially then – come to the cross and find communion with Jesus. Our drops of sorrow may be forgotten in the ocean of His griefs, but how high our love ought to rise!

Let that strong, deep love of Jesus flow into your soul like a stream flooding its banks. Let it flood all your faculties, drown all your sins, wash away your cares.

PERFUME FOR OUR SOULS

My lover is to me a sachet of myrrh.
Song of Songs 1:13

Why myrrh? It may be used here as a type of Jesus – on account of its preciousness, its perfume, its pleasantness, its healing, preserving, disinfecting qualities. But why a whole sachet of myrrh? First, the amount. There is enough in Christ for all my needs.

Second, for variety. Christ does not only meet a single need, but "in Christ all the fullness of the Deity lives in bodily form" (Col. 2:9). Everything we need is here. See Him in His virtue, gentleness, courage, self-denial, love, faithfulness, truth, and righteousness.

Finally, the sachet is set apart for a special purpose. So Jesus was set apart for His people. He gives His perfume only to those who enter into communion with Him, who come close to His presence.

CHRIST DESPISED OF MEN

All who see me mock me;
they hurl insults, shaking their heads.
Psalm 22:7

Mockery was a major ingredient in our Lord's sorrows. Judas mocked Him in the garden; the chief priests and scribes laughed Him to scorn; the servants and the soldiers jeered at Him and brutally insulted Him. And on the tree all sorts of horrid jests and hideous taunts were hurled at Him.

Imagine the Savior crucified, racked with anguish beyond all human apprehension. O Jesus, "despised and rejected by men" (Is. 53:3), how could You die for people who treated You so poorly? Here is love amazing, love divine, yes, love beyond degree.

We, too, have despised You in the past, and even since our rebirth we have given the world first place in our hearts. Yet You were dying to give us life.

FORSAKEN BY GOD

My God, my God, why have you forsaken me?
Psalm 22:1

No other moment at Calvary is so full of agony as this one. Christ suffered inexpressible spiritual agony, resulting from the departure of His Father's presence.

Sometimes we think we could cry, "My God, my God, why have You forsaken me?" There are seasons when the brightness of our Father's smile is eclipsed by clouds and darkness. But we must remember that God does never really forsake us – it only seems that way.

With Christ, it was a real forsaking. If you are a poor, distressed soul, who once lived in the sunshine of God's face, but are now in darkness, remember that He has not really forsaken you. God in the clouds is just as much our God as when He shines forth in all the luster of His grace.

THE PRECIOUS BLOOD

The precious blood of Christ.
1 Peter 1:19

Standing at the foot of the cross, we see hands, feet, and side, all pouring out crimson streams of precious blood. Why is it precious? Because it redeems us. By this blood, the sins of Christ's people are atoned for. We are redeemed from under the law. We are reconciled to God, made one with Him.

Christ's blood is also precious in its cleansing power. Although we have rebelled against our God, this blood allows us to stand before Him, accepted. The precious blood of Christ also sanctifies us. It not only takes away our sin, but also awakens our new nature and leads us on to follow God's commands. Ultimately, the blood is precious because of its overcoming power. The blood of Jesus! Sin dies in its presence; death is no longer death; heaven's gates are opened.

THE FOUNTAIN OF HIS BLOOD

The sprinkled blood that speaks
a better word than the blood of Abel.
Hebrews 12:24

Have you come to this sprinkled blood? I'm not asking if you have come to a knowledge of doctrine or the observance of ceremonies or some special experience, but have you come to the blood of Jesus?

The blood of Jesus gives life to godliness. To the repentant people of the earth, the shedding of Christ's blood is the music of heaven. We are full of sin, but as we gaze on the Savior's wounds, each drop of blood, as it falls, cries, "It is finished! I have put an end to sin!"

What sweet language this is! If you have come to that blood once, you will come constantly. You will feel your need to come to Him every day. It is a joy and privilege to wash in that fountain.

THE SCARLET CORD

And she tied the scarlet cord in the window.
Joshua 2:21

Rahab put her life in the hands of the spies. To her, they were representatives of the God of Israel.

Her faith was simple and firm, but it was very obedient. Tying the scarlet cord in the window was a very trivial act in itself, but she dared not forget it.

There is a solemn lesson in Rahab's simple act. Am I implicitly trusting in the precious blood of Jesus? Have I tied the scarlet cord in my window?

There is One who sees the scarlet line even when I lack the faith to see it myself. My Lord will see it and preserve me from His judgment.

THE TORN VEIL

At that moment the curtain of the temple
was torn in two from top to bottom.
The earth shook and the rocks split.
Matthew 27:51

This was no small miracle – the tearing of such a thick veil – but it was not intended merely as a display of power. It was a great object lesson for us. The old law was put aside. When Jesus died, the sacrifices were all fulfilled in Him. The tearing also revealed all the hidden things of the old system. The mercy seat could now be seen, and God's glory gleamed above it.

Access to God is now available to every believer in Christ Jesus. This is not one small peephole, through which we may peer at the mercy seat. No, this veil has been ripped apart, from top to bottom. We may come boldly to the throne of heavenly grace.

NO NEED TO FEAR

*So that by his death he might
destroy him who holds the power of death.*
Hebrews 2:14

Death has lost its sting, because the devil's power over it is destroyed. Then why are you afraid to die? Ask God to give you such a deep awareness of your Redeemer's death that you will be strengthened for that final hour.

Living near the cross of Calvary, you may think of death with pleasure and welcome it with intense delight when it comes.

It is a covenant blessing to "fall asleep" in Jesus. When the eyes close on earth, they open in heaven. So what is there for you to fear? The curse of death has been destroyed by our Lord. It is now only a "Jacob's ladder," with its foot in the dark grave, but its top reaching to eternal glory.

BLESSED ASSURANCE

I know that my Redeemer lives.
Job 19:25

The marrow of Job's comfort lies in that little word my – "my Redeemer" – and in the fact that his Redeemer lives. Oh, to get hold of a living Christ! Do not rest until you can say, by faith, "Yes, I throw myself upon my living Lord, and He is mine." Yet there is another word here that expresses Job's strong confidence: "I know." It is easy to say, "I hope so, I trust that ... " And there are thousands of Christians who never get much further. But to reach the essence of Christ's comfort, you must say, "I know."

Certainly if Job, in those ages before the coming of Christ, could say, "I know," we should not speak any less positively. A living Redeemer, truly mine, is joy unspeakable.

AWAITING GLORY

God exalted him.
Act 5:31

Jesus our Lord, once crucified, dead, and buried, now sits on the throne of glory. He has an undisputed right to the highest place that heaven affords.

Look up, believer, look to Jesus. Let the eye of your faith see Him with all His crowns, and remember that you will one day be like Him.

You will not be as great as He is, you will not be so divine, but you will, in some measure, share His honors and enjoy the same happiness and dignity that He has.

So be content to live unknown for now, and to walk your weary way through the fields of poverty or up the hills of affliction. Someday you will reign with Christ, for He has made us "kings and priests," and we will reign forever.

CONQUERING SIN

*No, in all these things we are more than
conquerors through him who loved us.*
Romans 8:37

We go to Christ for forgiveness, but all too often we look to the law for the power to fight our sins. Take your sins to Christ's cross, for our old nature can only be crucified there: We are crucified with Him. The only weapon to fight sin is the spear that pierced the side of Jesus.

Take your sin to Christ. Tell Him, "Lord, I have trusted You, and Your name is Jesus – for You save Your people from their sins. Lord, this is one of my sins. Save me from it!" Your prayers, your repentances, your tears – all of them put together – are worth nothing apart from Him. You must be conquerors through Him who has loved you, if you will be conquerors at all.

RENEWED COVENANTS

And because of all this we make a sure covenant.
Nehemiah 9:38 KJV

There are many times when we may renew our covenant with God. If He has crowned us with joy, we ought to crown Him again as our God. If we would learn to profit from our prosperity, we would not need so much adversity.

Have you recently received some blessing? Can you sing of the mercies God has blessed you with? Then this is the day to come to the altar, put yourself on it, and say, "I am yours, O Lord, fully and completely."

We need to be reminded regularly of God's promises to us. In the same way, we should renew our old vows, praying for God's strength to be true to them. This is a good time now. For the last month we have been considering Christ's sufferings. With gratitude, then, let us renew our "sure covenant" with the Lord.

THE VOICE OF THE BELOVED

Arise, my darling,
my beautiful one, and come with me.
Song of Songs 2:10

Listen! I hear the voice of my Beloved! He is speaking to me! "Come with Me," He beckons. Farther and farther from everything selfish, groveling, worldly, and sinful, He calls me. What possible reason would I have for staying in this wilderness of vanity and sin?

Lord, I want to come with You, but I am caught in these thorns and can't get away. If it were possible, I would like to have no heart for sin, no eyes or ears for sin. To come with You is to come home from exile, to come out of a raging storm, to come to the goal of my desires and the summit of my wishes. Draw me. Your grace can do it. Send Your Spirit to kindle sacred flames of love in my heart, and I will continue to rise until I leave life and time behind me and come to You.

FORGET HIM NOT

Do this in remembrance of me.
1 Corinthians 11:24

It would seem, from this verse, that Christians could forget Christ! How can those who have been redeemed by the blood of the dying Lamb and loved with an everlasting love ever forget their gracious Savior? You would think our memories would linger at the cross, but this cross is desecrated by the feet of forgetfulness.

Do you find yourself forgetting Jesus? Some other person or possession steals your heart, and you neglect the One who ought to have all your affection. Some earthly business engrosses your attention when you should fix your eyes steadily on the cross.

Let's bind a heavenly forget-me-not around our hearts for Jesus, our Beloved. Whatever else we may forget, let's hold fast to Him.

GOD IS ALL WE NEED

God, our God, will bless us.
Psalm 67:6

It is strange how little we make use of the spiritual blessings God gives us, but stranger how little we make use of God Himself. He is "our God," but we pay little attention to Him and ask Him few favors. We seldom even ask Him for advice. We go about our own business. In our troubles, we try to bear our own burdens, instead of casting them on the Lord. And it is not as if the Lord doesn't want to be bothered.

Learn the divine skill of making God everything to you. He can supply you with all things, but better yet, He can be all things to you. Make use of God in prayer, go to Him often. Whatever you are, wherever you are, remember God is there when you need Him; He is what you need and He is everything you need.

THE PROMISE OF THE WORD

*Remember your word to your servant,
for you have given me hope.*
Psalm 119:49

Whatever your special need may be, you will find some promise in the Bible suited to it. Do you feel weary because your life is so difficult? Here is the promise: "He gives strength to the weary and increases the power of the weak (Is. 40:29)." When you read a great promise like this, take it back to the Great Promiser and ask Him to keep His word.

Are you seeking after Christ, thirsting for a closer communion with Him? Don't ask for anything else, just go to God over and over again with this: "Lord, you have said it. Do what You have promised." Feast on God's own Word. Whatever your fears or wants, go to the bank of faith with your Father's handwritten check and say, "Remember Your word to Your servant, for You have given me hope."

DARK DAYS

You are my refuge in the day of disaster.
Jeremiah 17:17

The path of the Christian is not always bright with sunshine. We have times of darkness and storm. It is true that our religion is designed to give us happiness below as well as eternal bliss above. But experience tells us that at certain times clouds cover the believer's sun, and he walks in darkness. No Christian enjoys constant prosperity.

Perhaps the Lord gave you a smooth, bright path at first because you were weak and timid. But now that you are stronger in your spiritual life, you must encounter the riper, rougher experience of God's full-grown children. We need "disasters" to exercise our faith, to prune away the rotten branch of self-dependence and root us more firmly in Christ.

APRIL 30

THE FATHER'S CHASTENING

All the Israelites grumbled.
Numbers 14:2

There are grumblers among Christians now, just as there were in Israel's camp. There are those who cry out when God's rod of discipline falls on them. They ask, "Why am I being tormented like this?

What have I done to be disciplined this way?" What gives you the right to complain against our Lord's treatment of you? Certainly if He in His wisdom now decides to discipline you, you should not complain. Doesn't even your proud, rebellious spirit prove that your heart is not completely sanctified?

Certainly it should help you to deal with the chastening if you recognize your Father's hand in it, "because the Lord disciplines those he loves, and he punishes everyone he accepts as a son" (Heb. 12:6-7).

MAY

THE FRAGRANCE OF CHRIST

His cheeks are as a bed of spices, as sweet flowers.
Song of Songs 5:13 KJV

That cheek, which was once so harshly beaten, moistened with tears and then defiled with spittle – that cheek, as it smiles with mercy, brings rich fragrance to my heart.

Those cheeks were furrowed by the plow of grief and reddened with lines of blood from His thorn-crowned temples. Such marks of love charm my soul even more than perfume.

If I cannot see His whole face, at least let me see His cheeks, for even this glimpse of Him refreshes my spirit and yields a variety of delights.

In Jesus I find not only one flower, but a whole garden. He is my rose and lily. Precious Lord Jesus, let me know the blessedness that comes from abiding in unbroken fellowship with You.

SELFISH LONGINGS

*My prayer is not that you take them out of the world
but that you protect them from the evil one.*
John 17:15

Here we read of Christ praying that His people
would eventually be with Him, but He does not
ask that they be taken from the earth right away.
He wants them to stay here. Jesus did not plead
for our instant removal by death, because our
life on earth is important for others, if not for
ourselves.

Christians often want to die when they face
any trouble. I suspect that it is not so much their
longing to be with the Lord as it is their desire to
get rid of their troubles. Otherwise they would
feel the same wish to die when things are going
well. The wish to escape from trouble is a selfish
one. Instead, let your desire be to glorify God
by your life here, as long as He pleases. Let Him
say when it is enough.

STRENGTH IN DIFFICULTIES

In this world you will have trouble.
John 16:33

Do you wonder why this is? Look upward to your heavenly Father and see how pure and holy He is. Do you know that one day you will be like Him? Do you think that will really happen easily? Won't it take a great deal of refining in the furnace of affliction to purify you?

Then look around you. Where are you? In enemy territory. The world is not your friend. Finally, look within you, into your own heart. Sin and self are still inside you. You should expect trouble then.

But don't despair, God is with you to help and strengthen you. He has said, "I will be with you in trouble, I will deliver you and honor you" (see Ps. 91:15).

MODERN IDOLATRY

Do men make their own gods?
Yes, but they are not gods!
Jeremiah 16:20

One of the great besetting sins of Israel was idolatry, and the church – the spiritual Israel – is tempted in the same way. Mammon still puts up his golden calf, and the shrines of pride are well-kept. Self in various forms struggles to make believers slaves, and the flesh sets up altars wherever it can find space.

The objects of our foolish love are dubious blessings. The solace they offer us now is dangerous for us, and they give us little help in times of trouble. Why then are we so bewitched by these things? We should know better. We are committing two evils, forsaking the living God, and turning to idols. May the Lord purge us all from the worship of our modern idols.

GOD'S PEOPLE

I will be their God, and they will be my people.
2 Corinthians 6:16

How much meaning is couched in these two words: "My people." Here we find specialness. He has bought them with His own blood. He has loved them with an eternal love, a love that many waters cannot quench. Now can you see yourself as one of those chosen ones?

Can you look up to heaven and say, "My Lord and my God, You are mine because of the relationship You have established, entitling me to call You my Father; and You are mine by that holy fellowship we have when You reveal Yourself to me and I delight in Your presence"? If you can, then God says of you, and others like you, "My People."

For if God is your God, then the Lord loves you in a special way.

A HOUSE FOR YOUR SOUL

We live in Him.
1 John 4:13

Do you want a house for your soul? You may ask, "What is the purchase price?" It is less than proud human nature would like to pay. It is without money, without price. Will you take it on these terms? An eternal lease, nothing to pay, just the upkeep of loving and serving Him? Will you take Jesus and "live in Him"?

Look, this house is furnished with everything you could want. It is filled with riches more than you could spend as long as you live. Here you have intimate communion with Christ and feast on His love.

From this house, you can look out and see heaven itself. Here is the key: "Come to Jesus."

BELOVED PHYSICIAN

Many followed him, and he healed all their sick.
Matthew 12:15

In every corner of the field, Jesus was triumphant over evil and received acclaim of delivered captives. He came, He saw, He conquered everywhere. The same is true today. Whatever my own case may be, the beloved Physician can heal me.

Whatever may be the state of the others I am praying for, I have hope in Jesus that He will be able to heal them of their sins. However severe my struggle with sin and sicknesses, I can still rejoice.

He who walked among the sick on earth still dispenses His grace, and He still works wonders among us. I can go to Him with my need. The church on earth is full of souls healed by our beloved Physician. Then let us proclaim His grace far and wide.

KNOWING JESUS

The man who was healed had no idea who it was.
John 5:13

A great deal of ignorance of Jesus may remain in hearts that have felt His power. We should not condemn people for their lack of knowledge: If they have faith in Christ, we must assume salvation has been bestowed. The person who believes what he knows will soon know more clearly what he believes.

However, there is still danger in ignorance. This man was tormented by the Pharisees and was unable to cope with them. It is good to be able to answer our critics, but we cannot do so until we know the Lord Jesus well. This man found a cure for his ignorance: He was visited by the Lord, and later he was found testifying that "it was Jesus who had made him well" (v. 15).

ALL GOODNESS

*Who has blessed us with
every spiritual blessing in Christ.*
Ephesians 1:3

All the goodness of past, present, and future – this is what Christ gives His people. From all eternity, Jesus had the privileges of Sonship; and He has, by His gracious adoption and regeneration, elevated us to sonship as well, giving us "the right to become children of God" (Jn. 1:12).

We may rest assured that we are safe in Him. The marvelous incarnation of the God of heaven, in all its humble love, is ours.

We also have the blessings that come from perfect obedience, finished atonement, resurrection, ascension, and intercession. He has given us these things Himself. On His breastplate He wears our names. In His pleas before His Father's throne, He remembers our needs.

RESURRECTION LIFE

But Christ has indeed been raised from the dead.
1 Corinthians 15:20

The whole system of Christianity rests on the fact that Christ has been raised from the dead. For, "if Christ has not been raised, your faith is futile; you are still in your sins" (1 Cor. 15:17).

Our justification is linked with Christ's triumph over death and the grave. Our regeneration is connected with His rising. Finally, our ultimate resurrection rests here, for, "if the Spirit of him who raised Jesus from the dead is living in you, he who raised Christ from the dead will also give life to your mortal bodies through his Spirit, who lives in you" (Rom. 8:11).

So the silver thread of resurrection runs through all the believer's blessings, from his regeneration to his eternal glory, and it binds them all together. What a glorious fact it is that "Christ has indeed been raised from the dead"!

THE FIRM ROCK

I am with you always.
Matthew 28:20

There is Someone who is always the same and always with us. There is one stable Rock amid the turbulent waves of the sea of life.

Set your heart on the One who is always faithful to you. Do not build your house on the shifting quicksand of a deceitful world, but found your hopes upon this Rock, which stands firm despite pounding rain and roaring floods.

Trust yourself to the One who will go with you through the surging current of death's stream and land you safe on the celestial shore.

Entrust all your concerns to Him who can never be taken from you, who will never leave you, and who will never let you leave Him.

MAY 12

HUMILITY, HAPPINESS, HOLINESS

I will love him and show myself to him.
John 14:21

The Lord Jesus gives special revelations of Himself to His people. When Jesus reveals Himself to His people, it is heaven on earth, it is bliss begun. Such manifestations of Christ have a holy influence on the believer's heart.

One effect is humility. Another effect is happiness. In God's presence there are eternal pleasures. Holiness is sure to follow. A person without holiness has never had a special revelation of Christ. Some may claim a great deal, but we must not believe them until we see that their deeds match their words. So we see three results of being near to Jesus – humility, happiness and holiness. May God give them to you!

THE MORNING WILL COME

Weeping may remain for a night,
but rejoicing comes in the morning.
Psalm 30:5

If you are in a trial, think of tomorrow. Cheer up your heart with the thought of the Lord's coming. Be patient! Think how trivial our troubles will seem when we look back on them!

As we look at them now, they seem immense, but when we get to heaven, our trials will seem like light and momentary afflictions. So let us move on boldly.

Even if the night is darker than it has ever been, the morning is coming. Do you know how to anticipate the joys of heaven, to live in expectation? It is a comforting hope.

It may be dark now, but the morning brings light. Our weeping will turn to rejoicing.

A SHARE IN HIS INHERITANCE

Heirs of God and co-heirs with Christ.
Romans 8:17

The unlimited realms of the Father's universe belong to Christ. As God's Son, He is the heir to this fortune, the sole proprietor of the vast creation. He has allowed us to claim the whole estate as ours, too, since we have officially been named as co-heirs with Him. Here is the reward for every Christian conqueror! Christ's throne, crown, scepter, palace, treasure, robes, and heritage are yours.

The smiles of His Father were all the sweeter to Him because His people were sharing them. The honors of His kingdom are more pleasing, because His people will appear with Him in glory. His conquests are more valuable, because they have taught His people to overcome. He delights in His throne, because there is a place on it for them.

PRESENT JUSTIFICATION

Everyone who believes is justified.
Acts 13:39

A person who believes in Christ receives a present justification. Faith produces this fruit now, not at some distant time. Justification is given to the soul at the moment when it accepts Christ as its all in all. Today we are absolved from sin. Today we are acquitted in God's court.

Now we are pardoned. Now our sins are put away. Now we stand accepted before God, as if we had not been guilty. "Therefore, there is now no condemnation for those who are in Christ Jesus" (Rom. 8:1).

There is not a single sin in God's Book, even now, against any of God's people. Who dares to accuse them? Let our present privilege awaken us to present duty. Now, while life lasts, let us spend and be spent for our sweet Lord Jesus.

ABUNDANT GRACE

*God richly provides us
with everything for our enjoyment.*
1 Timothy 6:17

Our Lord Jesus is always giving to us. As long as there is a vessel of grace that is not yet full to the brim, He will not stop pouring the oil of His blessing. He is an ever-shining sun. He is manna that is constantly falling around the camp. He is a Rock in the desert, always sending out streams of life from His smitten side.

The rain of His grace is always pouring down; the river of His blessing flows on and on; and the wellspring of His love overflows endlessly.

Who has ever returned from His door unblessed? Who has ever risen from His table unsatisfied? His mercies are new every morning and fresh every evening. Who can count all His benefits? How can my soul ever praise Him enough?

THE FOOTSTEPS OF JESUS

*Whoever claims to live in him
must walk as Jesus did.*
1 John 2:6

If Christians want their souls to be healthy, if they want to avoid the sickness of sin and enjoy the vigor of growing grace, they should let Jesus be their model.

For their own happiness, if they want the finest in life, if they want to enjoy holy and happy communion with Jesus, if they want to be lifted above the cares and troubles of this world, then let them walk as Jesus walked. When you are enabled, by the Holy Spirit, to walk in the very footsteps of Jesus, you show yourself to be a child of God.

But especially for Christ's own sake, follow His example. Do you love your Savior? Is His name precious to you? Do you want Him to be glorified? Be a letter from Christ that is "known and read by everybody" (2 Cor. 3:2-3).

THE FULLNESS OF CHRIST

*For in Christ all the fullness of the Deity
lives in bodily form, and you have
been given fullness in Christ, who is the
head over every power and authority.*
Colossians 2:9-10

All the attributes of Christ, as God and Man, are at our disposal. All the fullness of the Deity is ours to make us complete. His omnipotence, omniscience, omnipresence, immutability, and infallibility are all combined for our defense.

The fathomless love of the Savior's heart is ours – every drop. All of Christ in His adorable character as the Son of God, is granted to us for our enjoyment. His wisdom directs us, His knowledge instructs us, His power protects us, His justice upholds us, and His love comforts us. He holds nothing back. "Ah, all, all, are yours," He says. "Be satisfied with My grace and be full of My goodness."

SERVANTS AND KINGS

I have seen slaves on horseback,
while princes go on foot like slaves.
Ecclesiastes 10:7

When our Lord was on earth, although He was the Prince of the kings of the earth, yet He walked the paths of weariness and service – a Servant of servants. We should not be surprised if His followers should also be looked down upon.

We must not let our passions and carnal appetites ride in triumph, while our nobler instincts walk in the dust. Grace must reign in our lives as a prince, making the members of our bodies its servants.

We were not created to allow our passions to rule over us, but so that we, as kings, might reign with Christ over our spirits, souls, and bodies, to the glory of God the Father.

OFFERINGS OF THE HEART

Show the wonder of your great love.
Psalm 17:7

When we give our offerings, do we also give our hearts? We often fail in this respect, but the Lord never does. His favors always come to us with the love of His heart. He does not send us the leftovers and crumbs from His dining table, but He dips our morsel in His own dish and seasons our meals with the spices of His fragrant affection.

He gives freely and there is no hint that we are a burden to Him. He rejoices in His mercy and presses us close to Him as He pours out His life for us.

What a special communion this is: May we continually taste it and know its blessedness.

BEYOND THE IFS

If ye have tasted that the Lord is gracious.
1 Peter 2:3 KJV

"If" – there is a possibility, even a probability that some have not tasted that the Lord is gracious. No one ought to be content as long as there is an "if" about his having tasted that the Lord is gracious.

A zealous and holy distrust of self may create a momentary doubt in the believer's heart, but the continuing of such a doubt would be an awful thing.

Do not rest, believer, until you have a full assurance of where you stand with Jesus. Do not let anything satisfy you, until, as the Holy Spirit bears witness with your spirit, you are convinced that you are a child of God.

Don't be satisfied with perhaps or if or maybe. Build on eternal sureties and build on them surely.

THE TESTING OF YOUR FAITH

He led them by a straight way.
Psalm 107:7

Experiencing great changes, the anxious believer might sometimes ask, "Why am I going through this?" Is this part of God's plan for me? Is this any way for God to bring me toward heaven?

Yes, it is. The eclipse of your faith, the darkness of your mind, the fainting of your hope – all these things are just parts of God's method of making you ripe for the great inheritance you will soon receive. These trials are for the strengthening and the testing of your faith. By these things is the life of your soul maintained.

Each of these helps you on your way. "We must go through many hardships to enter the kingdom of God," (Acts 14:22). So learn to "consider it pure joy" (Jas. 1:2).

CONFIDENCE IN THE LORD

The LORD will fulfill his purpose for me.
Psalm 138:8

The psalmist did not say, "I have grace enough to fulfill God's purposes for me." No, his dependence was on the Lord alone. If we indulge in any confidence that is not grounded on the Rock of Ages, our confidence is worse than a dream – it will fall on us and cover us with its ruins, causing sorrow and confusion.

The psalmist was wise. He rested on nothing short of the Lord's work. It is the Lord who has begun a good work in us, and He has carried it on. If He does not finish it, no one will. But this is our confidence: He has done it all, must do it all, and will do it all.

Our confidence must not be in what we have done or in what we have resolved to do, but entirely in what the Lord will do. Thanks be to God, He will fulfill His purposes for us.

PERSEVERING PRAYER

Praise be to God, who has not rejected my prayer!
Psalm 66:20

If we honestly look at the character of our prayers, we would be surprised that God ever answers them. Some may think that their prayers are worthy of acceptance. But the true Christian looks more humbly at his prayers. Your requests have been faint and few, far removed from that persevering faith that cries, "I will not let You go unless You bless me!" (Gen. 32:26). Yet strange as it may seem, God has heard these cold prayers of yours – and not only heard, but answered them. It is strange and wonderful that God should pay attention to these intermittent spasms of prayer that come and go according to our immediate needs.

Oh, may our hearts be touched by His gracious kindness, so that we may "pray in the Spirit on all occasions with all kinds of prayers and requests" (Eph. 6:18).

THE PRESENCE OF THE LORD

O LORD, do not forsake me.
Psalm 38:21

We often pray that God will not forsake us in our times of trial and temptation, but we forget that we need to pray like this at all times. There is no moment in our lives in which we can do without His constant upholding.

So let this be your prayer today: "Do not forsake me, Lord, now or at any moment of my life. Forsake me not in my joys, lest they absorb my heart. Forsake me not in my sorrows, lest I complain against You. Forsake me not in the time when my faith is strongest, lest faith degenerate into presumption. Without You, Lord, I am weak. With You, I am strong. Do not forsake me, for my path is dangerous. I cannot do without Your guidance.

As the hen will not forsake her brood, so cover me forever with Your feathers, let me find refuge under Your wings."

DO NOT BE ANXIOUS

Cast your cares on the LORD and he will sustain you.
Psalm 55:22

Care can be sinful – even when we are caring about legitimate things – if it is carried to extremes. Our Savior regularly taught that we should avoid anxious concern.

The very essence of anxious care is imagining that we are wiser than God. When we worry, we put ourselves in His place and try to do for Him what He intends to do for us. We struggle to bear our burden, as if He were unable or unwilling to carry it for us. Anxiety makes us doubt God's loving-kindness, and so our love for Him grows cold.

As a result, our prayers are hindered, our consistent example is marred, and our lives become self-seeking. But if, through simple faith in His promise, we cast each burden upon Him, we will remain close to Him, strengthened against temptation.

THE FATHER'S KINDNESS

And Mephibosheth lived in Jerusalem,
because he always ate at the king's table,
and he was crippled in both feet.
2 Samuel 9:13

This is the kind of love the Father has for His only begotten Son, that for His sake, He raises His lowly brothers from poverty and banishment to noble rank and royal provisions. The Lord blesses us with His friendship because He sees in us the righteousness of His dearly beloved Jesus.

Our deformity does not rob us of our privileges. Our "might" may limp, but our "right" does not. At the Lord's table we learn to glory in our infirmities, because the power of Christ rests upon us.

Lord, help the lame to leap like a deer. Satisfy all your people with the bread of Your table!

IN A LITTLE WHILE

Those he justified, he also glorified.
Romans 8:30

Here is a precious truth for you, believer. You may be poor or suffering, but it may encourage you to review your "calling" and the consequences that flow from it. As surely as you are God's child, your trials will soon end, and you will bask in His riches. Wait a while, and your weary head will wear a crown of glory, your laboring hand will grab the palm branch of victory.

If He has called you, nothing can divide you from His love. Distress cannot sever the bond. The fire of persecution cannot burn the ropes that bind you to Him. You are secure. Rest assured, the heart of your Justifier beats with an infinite love for you. Soon you will be with the glorified. You are only waiting here to prepare for your inheritance.

WICKEDNESS

You hate wickedness.
Psalm 45:7

There can be hardly any goodness in a person if he does not hate wickedness. If he loves truth, he must despise every false way.

Our Lord Jesus hated wickedness so much that He bled in order to deal it a deathblow. He died so that it might die. And He rose so that He might trample it under His feet.

Wickedness dresses up in fine clothes and imitates the language of holiness. But the teachings of Jesus, like His famous whip, chase it out of the temple – and will not tolerate it in the church. When our Redeemer comes in judgment, He will reveal His eternal abhorrence of iniquity with the words "Depart form Me, you who are cursed!" As warm as His love is toward sinners, so hot is His hatred for sin.

LITTLE SINS

Catch for us the foxes, the little foxes that ruin the vineyards, our vineyards that are in bloom.
Song of Songs 2:15

A little thorn may cause much suffering. A little cloud may hide the sun. Little foxes ruin the vineyards. And little sins do mischief to the tender heart. These little sins burrow into the soul, filling it with things that Christ hates, so that He cannot have comfortable fellowship with us.

Sadly, some Christians seldom enjoy their Savior's presence. So think about it. What has driven Christ away from you? He hides His face behind the wall of your sins. That wall may be built of little pebbles.

If you want to live with Christ, watch out for "the little foxes that ruin the vineyards."

THE VALLEY OF AFFLICTION

The king also crossed the Kidron Valley.
2 Samuel 15:23

It should comfort us to know that Jesus has been tempted in every way that we are. What is our Kidron this morning? Is it a treacherous friend, a sad bereavement, a slanderous attack, a dark sense of foreboding? The King has gone through all of these. Is it bodily pain, poverty, persecution, or contempt? The King has crossed each of these Kidrons before us.

We must banish once and for all the idea that our afflictions are unique, because Jesus has been through them all.

Courage, soldiers of the cross, the King Himself triumphed after going through Kidron, and so will you.

JUNE

NIGHT AND DAY

*And there was evening, and there
was morning – the first day.*
Genesis 1:5

Was it true even from the beginning? Did light
and darkness divide the realm of time in the first
day? Then it is little wonder that my life also
changes between the sunshine of prosperity and
the midnight of adversity. There will not always
be the blaze of noon in my soul. At times I must
expect to mourn the loss of previous joys and to
seek my Beloved in the night.

Praise the Lord for the sun of joy when it rises
and for the gloom of evening as it falls. There is
beauty in both sunrise and sunset. Sing of it and
glorify the Lord. Then believe that the night is as
useful as the day. The dews of grace fall heavily
in the night of sorrow. The stars of promise shine
gloriously in the darkness of grief.

FIERCE BATTLES

For the sinful nature desires what is
contrary to the Spirit, and the Spirit
what is contrary to the sinful nature.
Galatians 5:17

In every believer's heart there is a constant struggle between the old nature and the new. But although the battle is often fierce, we have a mighty helper – Jesus, the captain of our salvation. He is always with us, and He assures us that we will end up as "more than conquerors" through Him.

Are you fighting with the enemy today? Have Satan, the world, and your sinful nature all lined up against you? Do not be discouraged or dismayed. God Himself is with you. So do not be afraid.

Who can defeat the All-powerful One? You will overcome. Keep fighting, "looking unto Jesus." The conflict may be long and intense, but the victory will be sweet, and the promised reward is glorious.

SERVICE FOR THE KING

*These were the potters, and those that
dwelt among plants and hedges:
there they dwelt with the king for his work.*
1 Chronicles 4:23 KJV

We, too, may be engaged in the most menial part of the Lord's work, but it is a great privilege to do anything for "the king." We are what we are. We should not let whims or fancies move us this way or that, but we should seek to serve the Lord where we are, by being a blessing to those around us.

You unknown workers who are busy for Your Lord in the middle of the dirt and misery of the lowest of the low, rejoice! Earthen pots get filled with heavenly treasure. Stay close to the king in whatever work you do, and when He writes the chronicles, your name will be recorded.

JUNE 4

AMAZING LOVE

The kindness and love of God our Savior.
Titus 3:4

When we consider the history of the Redeemer's love, we recall a thousand enchanting acts of affection. Each of these weaves our hearts with Christ's, twisting together the thoughts and emotions of our renewed souls with the mind of Jesus.

When we meditate on this amazing love, we may even faint with joy. To consider that great Benefactor of the church endowing her with all His wealth – who can comprehend such weighty love?

The Holy Spirit sometimes gives us a partial sense of the magnitude of divine love, but our souls even have a hard time containing that! How staggering it would be to see it in its fullness!

THE ARK OF SAFETY

Then the LORD shut him in.
Genesis 7:16

Noah was shut away from the world by the hand of divine love. God intentionally separates us from the world, which lies in the domain of the evil one.

We are not of the world, just as our Lord Jesus was not of the world. We cannot follow the sinful pursuits of the multitude.

Outside the ark, it was all ruined, but inside there was rest and peace. Without Christ, we perish. But in Christ Jesus there is perfect safety.

Those who are in Christ Jesus are in Him forever. Eternal faithfulness has shut them in, and no amount of devilish malice can drag them out.

JUST AS YOU ARE

I am unworthy.
Job 40:4

This is actually a comforting thought for the humble sinner. You may think that you cannot approach God because you are so unworthy, but there is not a saint on earth who has not felt unworthy.

If Job and Isaiah and Paul were all obliged to say they were unworthy, will you be ashamed to join in the same confession?

If God loves His people when they are unworthy, do you think your unworthiness will prevent Him from loving you?

Put your faith in Jesus! Jesus wants you just as you are. Oh, may the Holy Spirit give you a saving faith in the One who welcomes the unworthy.

HATING EVIL

Let those who love the LORD hate evil.
Psalm 97:10

You have good reason to "hate evil." Consider what harm it has already done to you. Sin blinded you so that you could not see the Savior's beauty. Sin directed your feet into the pathway of death and poisoned the very fountain of your being. Our souls would have been lost if God's all-powerful love had not stepped in.

If you truly love your Savior and want to honor Him, then "hate evil." How? There is no better cure for the love of evil in a Christian than intimate fellowship with the Lord Jesus.

Live close to Him, and it will be impossible for you to be at peace with sin.

THE LORD'S BATTLE

Many others fell slain, because the battle was God's.
1 Chronicles 5:22

If the battle is God's, the victory is sure. We must go forth in the Lord's name. The biblical fighters carried shields, swords, and bows, but they did not put their trust in these weapons. In the same way, we must use all proper methods in our struggles, but our confidence must rest in God alone. He is the sword and shield of His people.

Friends, as we fight against sin in our lives and in society, against errors both doctrinal and practical, against spiritual wickedness in high places and low, we are waging God's battle! We need not fear defeat. Do not be cowed by difficulties, do not flinch at wounds, or even death. Attack with the two-edged sword of the Spirit, and you will prevail. With steadfast feet, a strong hand, a fearless heart, and flaming zeal, rush into battle, and the hosts of evil will fly like chaff in the wind.

A HEALTHY SOUL

The LORD has done great things for us,
and we are filled with joy.
Psalm 126:3

Some Christians are sadly prone to look on the dark side of everything. They dwell more on what they have gone through than on what God has done for them. But a Christian whose soul is in a healthy state will come forward joyously and say, "Let me tell you what the Lord has done in my life."

It is true that we endure trials, but it is just as true that we are delivered out of them. It is true that we have sins that we are sorry for, but we also have an all-sufficient Savior who overcomes these sins and keeps us out of their power. It would be wrong to deny that we have problems. But it would be just as wrong to forget that we come through our problems, thanks to our Almighty Helper.

GLORIFY CHRIST

We live to the Lord.
Romans 14:8

It is true that our sanctification is a long process, and we will not be perfected until we lay aside our bodies and enter glory. But still, if the Lord wanted to, He could have changed us immediately from imperfection to perfection. Why then are we still here? Would God keep His children out of Paradise a single moment longer than was necessary?

The answer is: We are here so that we may "live to the Lord" and bring others to know His love.

We remain on earth as sowers to scatter good seed, as plowmen to break up the fallow ground, as messengers to proclaim salvation.

We are here to glorify Christ in our daily lives, we are here as workers for Him, and as workers together with Him.

LOVE BEGETS LOVE

We love because he first loved us.
1 John 4:19

Anyone can have a cold admiration when studying God's works, but the warmth of love is kindled in our hearts only by God's Spirit. It is incredible that we could ever be brought to love Jesus at all. We rebelled against Him – it is amazing that He would want to draw us back.

But even after God's love is born in our hearts, it must be nourished by Him. Love is an exotic plant; it does not grow naturally in human soil. It must be specially watered from above. If it receives no nourishment except what it can draw from our rocky hearts, it will soon wither. It requires heavenly nourishment. It cannot exist in the wilderness unless it receives God's manna.

Love must feed on love. The very soul of our love for God is His love for us.

THE SCALE OF GOD'S WORD

*You have been weighed on
the scales and found wanting.*
Daniel 5:27

We should frequently weigh ourselves on the scale of God's Word. You may find it helpful to turn to the life of Christ. As you read, ask yourself how closely you conform to His image.

Determine whether you have the meekness, the humility, the loving spirit that He constantly displayed. Then turn to the epistles and see whether you can go along with what the apostle says about his experience.

If we read God's Word in this way as a test of our spiritual condition, we may stop every so often and say, "Lord, I feel that I haven't yet been here. Bring me here! Give me true repentance, real faith, warmer zeal, more fervent love – as I read about here. Make me more like Jesus. I don't want to be 'found wanting' anymore."

THE FREE GIFT

*And whoever wishes, let him
take the free gift of the water of life.*
Revelation 22:17

Jesus says, "Take freely." He wants no payment. He seeks no special favors. If you are willing, you are invited. So come! He gives Himself to those who need Him.

How many are there who are rich in their own good works and therefore will not come to Christ? "I refuse to be saved," they say, "in the same way as prostitutes and garbage collectors." But is there any other pathway to glory except that path that led the dying thief there? No. No one will be saved in any other way.

Such proud boasters may remain without the living water, but "whoever wishes, let him take the free gift of the water of life."

DELIGHT IN HOLINESS

Delight yourself in the Lord.
Psalm 37:4

The believer's life is described here as a delight in God, so we are reminded that true religion overflows with happiness and joy.

The thought of delight in religion is so strange to most people that they can't think of two words further apart in meaning than holiness and delight. But believers who know Christ understand that delight and faith are united. Nothing can separate the two.

Those who love God with all their hearts find that His ways are ways of pleasantness and all His paths are peace.

The saints find such joys, such brimming delights, such overflowing blessedness in the Lord that serving Him is no mere custom. Our piety is our pleasure; our hope is our happiness; our duty is our delight.

A SEA OF JOY

Sarah said, "God has brought me laughter, and everyone who hears about this will laugh with me."
Genesis 21:6

It was far beyond the laws of nature that the aged Sarah should be honored with a son. In the same way, it is beyond all ordinary rules that I, a poor helpless, undone sinner, should bear in my soul the Spirit of Jesus. Yet I have been enabled to bring forth fruit unto holiness.

Yes, my mouth should be filled with joyous laughter, because of this surprising grace that I have received from the Lord.

The Lord Jesus is a deep sea of joy. My soul will dive into it and will be swallowed up in the delights of His companionship.

When my soul looks at Jesus, I want heaven and earth to unite in joy unspeakable.

BANISH DOUBT

I give them eternal life, and they shall never perish.
John 10:28

For a child of God to mistrust his Father's love, truth, and faithfulness must be greatly displeasing to the Lord. How could we ever doubt His upholding grace? Christ Himself said, "I give them eternal life, and they shall never perish; no one can snatch them out of my Father's hand" (Jn. 10:28).

If His love could fail, these promises would be false. God could no longer claim to be true, honorable, all-powerful, gracious, and promise keeping if any of those for whom Christ has died and who have put their trust in Him should be cast away.

Banish those doubting fears that dishonor God. Get up, shake off the dust, and put on your beautiful garments of faith. Let the eternal life within you express itself in constant rejoicing.

A POWERFUL PRAYER

Help, Lord.
Psalm 12:1

This prayer itself is remarkable, for it is short, but seasonable. It expresses the deep sentiments of the psalmist, and it suggests that the Lord is strong enough to help. These two words are direct, clear, and distinctive. They say much more than many of us do in our rambling outpourings. The psalmist runs straight to God. He knows what he wants and where to get it.

We can find many occasions to use this simple prayer. The answer to this prayer is certain, if the prayer is sincerely offered through Jesus. The Lord has promised that He will not leave His people. He guarantees His aid: "Do not fear, I will help you" (Is. 41:13).

OUR LORD JESUS CHRIST

Your Redeemer.
Isaiah 54:5

Jesus, our Redeemer, is thoroughly ours – and He is ours forever. All the offices of Christ are held on our behalf. He is King for us, Priest for us, and Prophet for us.

But His humanity is also ours in all its perfection. Our gracious Lord offers to us the spotless virtue of His stainless character. He gives us the reward He won for His obedient submission and loyal service.

The unsullied garment of His life covers us with beauty. The glittering virtues of His character are our jewels. And the superhuman meekness of His death is our boast and glory.

All His thoughts, emotions, actions, sayings, miracles, and prayers were for us. Christ is in every way our Christ, for us to enjoy richly forever.

THE HOLY SPIRIT

All of them were filled with the Holy Spirit.
Acts 2:4

The blessings of this day were rich. It is impossible to estimate the full consequences of this sacred filling of the soul. Life, comfort, light, purity, power, peace and many other precious blessings – all these go along with the Savior's presence.

As fire, He purges away our impurities and sets a holy fire inside us. He is the sacrificial flame, enabling us to offer our whole selves as a living sacrifice to God. He descends upon His chosen ones as He fell upon Jesus in the Jordan and testifies that they are God's children by developing within them a spirit to cry, "Abba, Father."

As the wind, He breathes life into people, blowing where He wants to, animating and sustaining all creation. May we feel His presence today and every day.

SHAKEN GRAIN

*For I will give the command, and I will
shake the house of Israel among all the
nations as grain is shaken in a sieve,
and not a pebble will reach the ground.*
Amos 9:9

Every sifting comes by divine command or permission. The overruling hand of the Master is purifying the grain in the very same process that the enemy intends as a destructive measure.

If you feel like grain on the Lord's floor that has been sifted again and again, take comfort from the fact that the Lord is ultimately in charge of the sieve. He is using it for His glory and for your eternal profit. Observe the complete safety of God's grain.

Every individual believer is precious in the Lord's sight. The Lord will not lose one of His redeemed people. However little we may be, if we are the Lord's, we may rejoice that we are preserved in Christ Jesus.

SPLENDID IN BEAUTY

You are the most excellent of men.
Psalm 45:2

The entire person of Jesus is like a single jewel. He is complete, not only in His various aspects, but as a gracious, all-glorious whole. He is, in total, a picture of beauty. He is perfectly and altogether lovely.

O Jesus! Your power, Your grace, Your justice, Your tenderness, Your truth, Your majesty, and Your immutability combine to make up such a man that neither heaven nor earth have seen elsewhere. As all the colors blend into one resplendent rainbow, so all the glories of heaven and earth meet in You and unite so wondrously that there is no one to compare with You. Your fragrance is a holy scent that the best perfumer could never match. Each spice is fragrant, but the compound is divine.

LIVING STONES

*It is he who will build the temple of the LORD,
and he will be clothed with majesty.*
Zechariah 6:13

Christ Himself is the builder of His spiritual temple, and He has built it on the mountains of His unchanging affection, His omnipotent grace, and His infallible truthfulness. But just as in Solomon's temple, the materials still need to be prepared.

There are the rough stones still in the quarry. These must be cut out and squared. All of this is Christ's own work. Each individual believer is being prepared and polished, made ready for his place in the temple.

Our prayers and efforts cannot make us ready for heaven, apart from the hand of Jesus, who is fashioning our hearts the way He wants them.

EVENLY BAKED

Ephraim is a flat cake not turned over.
Hosea 7:8

A cake not turned is uncooked on one side. Each of us should consider whether this is our own case. Are we thoroughly devoted to God? While there is a long way to grow, we should be growing evenly. If there is holiness in part of our lives while sin reigns in another, then we are also "a flat cake not turned over."

A cake not turned over is soon burned on the side nearest the fire. Although no one can have too much religion, there are some who seem burned black with bigoted zeal for one part of the truth while neglecting others. The saint in public is a devil in private. He deals in flour by day and in soot by night. The cake is burned on one side and doughy on the other. If this is the way I am Lord, please turn my unsanctified nature to the fire of Your love.

HEARING AND OBEYING

As Jesus was saying these things, a woman in the crowd called out, "Blessed is the mother who gave you birth and nursed you." He replied, "Blessed rather are those who hear the word of God and obey it."
Luke 11:27-28

Some people fondly imagine that it must have involved very special privileges to have been the mother of our Lord. We don't know that Mary knew more than others. What she did know, she properly stored up in her heart. Everything that she knew we may discover too.

The Divine Revealer of Secrets tells us everything that is in His heart, everything that we need to know. Even today He is revealing Himself to you. So you don't need to cry out, "Blessed is the woman who bore you!" Instead, you can bless the Lord for giving you the privilege of hearing His Word and obeying it. That gives us just as close a relationship with Jesus and just as thorough a knowledge as Mary would have had.

HIGH PLACES

Go up on a high mountain.
Isaiah 40:9

Our knowledge of Christ is something like climbing a mountain. When you are at the base, you see only a little bit. Keep climbing, and the scene enlarges, until at last you are on the summit.

Now the Christian life is of the same order. When we first believe in Christ, we only see a bit of Him. The higher we climb, the more we discover of His beauties. The gray-haired Paul, shivering in a dungeon in Rome, could say, "I know whom I have believed" (2 Tim. 1:12), for each of his experiences was like the climbing of a hill, and his approaching death was like reaching the top. From there he could see the entire panorama of the faithfulness and love of the One to whom he had committed his soul.

MAKING SURE

You have become like us.
Isaiah 14:10

Consider the tragedy of the person who professes Christianity but doesn't truly believe. No greater eagerness will ever be seen among the tormentors of hell than when devils drag a hypocrite's soul down to destruction.

John Bunyan wrote about the "back door" to hell. Watch out for that. "Examine yourselves to see whether you are in the faith" (2 Cor. 13:5). Look deeply at your situation. Are you in Christ? It is the easiest thing in the world to give a lenient verdict when you are putting yourself on trial. But be fair and true here.

If your house is not built on the rock, it will fall, and its fall will be great. May the Lord give you sincerity, consistency, and firm commitment.

SEPARATION FROM THE WORLD

But you must not go very far.
Exodus 8:28

The world wants us to be more compromising and not to take our faith to an extreme. The ideas of "dying to the world" and "being buried with Christ" seem ridiculous to carnal minds. Worldly wisdom speaks of "moderation." According to this principle, purity may be desirable, but let's not get too precise about it. Of course, they say, truth should be followed, but one should never denounce error too severely.

If we want to follow the Lord thoroughly, we must depart immediately for the wilderness of separation, leaving the Egypt of the carnal world behind us. The farther you are from a deadly viper, the better. The same is true of worldly conformity – stay away!

LOOK TO CHRIST

Let us fix our eyes on Jesus.
Hebrews 12:2

The Holy Spirit is always working to turn our eyes from ourselves to Jesus. But Satan's work is just the opposite: he is always trying to get us to think of ourselves instead of Christ. The Holy Spirit turns our eyes entirely away from self.

Remember, it is not your hold on Christ that saves you – it is Christ. So don't look at your own hand trying to grasp Christ. Look to Christ. Don't look to your own hope, but to Jesus, the source of your hope. Don't look at your faith, but to Jesus, the "author and perfecter of our faith" (Heb. 12:2).

It is what Jesus is, not what we are, that gives rest to the soul. Don't let your hopes and fears come between you and Jesus. Follow Him closely, and He will never fail you.

AWAKE TO LIFE

*God will bring with Jesus those
who have fallen asleep in him.*
1 Thessalonians 4:14

The idea connected with sleep is "rest," and that is the idea the Spirit wants to convey to us. Sleep makes each night a Sabbath for the day. Sleep shuts the door of the soul and keeps all visitors out for a while, so that the inner life may enjoy its garden of ease. The hardworking believer sleeps quietly, as does the weary child on its mother's breast.

In the same way, those who die in the Lord are happy. They rest from their labors, and their works follow them. Imagine their awakening! Weary and worn, they were laid to rest, but they will wake up in beauty and glory. The shriveled seed rises from the dust as a beautiful flower. The winter of the grave gives way to the spring of redemption and the summer of glory.

AN ENDLESS SUPPLY

"I have given them the glory that you gave me."
John 17:22

How great is the generosity of Jesus! He has given us His all. Even if He only donated a tenth of His possessions to our cause, it would make us rich beyond belief. But He was not content until He had given everything.

If He had merely allowed us to eat the crumbs of blessing that fell from the table of His mercy, that would be amazing grace. But He will do nothing by halves. He invites us to sit with Him and share the feast.

The boundless depth of His all-sufficiency is as free to the believer as the air we breathe. Christ has lifted the goblet of love and grace to our lips and asks us to drink. We will never exhaust the supply.

JULY

STREAMS OF LIVING WATER

*On that day living water will
flow in summer and in winter.*
Zechariah 14:8

The streams of living water that flow from Jerusalem are not dried up by the parching heat of the sultry summer, nor are they frozen by the blustery winds of winter.

The seasons change – and you change – but your Lord is always the same. The streams of His love are as deep, as broad, as full as ever.

At any time I can go and drink from this inexhaustible fountain – it pours forth blessings in summer and winter.

The beds of ancient rivers have been found, all dry and desolate, but the streams that flow from the mountains of divine sovereignty and infinite love will always be full to the brim. Generations melt away, but the course of grace is unaltered.

SINGING IN THE STORM

In him our hearts rejoice.
Psalm 33:21

Christians can rejoice even in the deepest distress. Though trouble may surround them, they still sing. The waves may roll over them, but their souls soon rise to the surface and see the light of God's face. They have a buoyancy about them that keeps their heads above water and helps them sing in the middle of the storm, "God is with me still!"

Trouble does not necessarily bring comfort along with it; it is the presence of the Son of God in the fiery furnace with him that fills the believer's heart with joy. The Christian may be sick and suffering, but Jesus visits him. The believer is not afraid to die. He has seen Jesus as the morning star, and he longs to gaze upon Him as the sun in all His strength. Truly, the presence of Jesus is all the heaven we desire.

BEING NOURISHED IN GOD

*And the cows that were ugly and
gaunt ate up the seven sleek, fat cows.*

Genesis 41:4

I need to beware of "ugly and gaunt" prayers, praises, duties, and experiences. They will eat up the fat of my comfort and peace. If I neglect prayer for even a short time, I lose all the spirituality I had attained. If I draw no fresh supplies from heaven, the old corn in my silo is soon consumed by the famine in my soul.

The only way all my days can be sleek and fat is to feed them in the right meadow, that is, to spend these days with the Lord, in His service, in His company, in His way.

Why shouldn't every day be richer than the day before – in love, in usefulness, in joy? O Lord, may I be nourished in Your house, so that I may praise Your name.

THE TRUTH

Sanctify them by the truth.
John 17:17

Sanctification begins in regeneration. The Spirit of God infuses into a person the new living principle that makes him a "new creation" (2 Cor. 5:17) in Christ Jesus. This process is carried on every day as the Christian is preserved in God's grace. The Spirit helps the Christian abound in good works, for the glory of God. But, there is another factor involved.

"Sanctify them," Jesus prayed, "by the truth; your word is truth." The Spirit of God brings to our minds the precepts and doctrines of truth, and applies them with power. The truth is our sanctifier. If we do not hear or read it, we will not grow in sanctification. We only progress in sound living as we progress in sound understanding. Hold tightly to the truth; in this way you will be sanctified by the Spirit of God.

BEING SAINTS

Called to be saints.
Romans 1:7

We tend to regard the apostles as if they were "saints" in some special way. Each person whom God has called by His grace and sanctified by His Spirit is a saint.

Do not look on the ancient saints as being exempt from weakness or sin. Their holiness is something that we, too, can attain. We are "called to be saints" by the same voice that called them. If these saints accomplished more than we have – and they did – then let's emulate their ardor and holiness.

They lived with Jesus, they lived for Jesus, and so they grew to be like Jesus. Let us live by the same Spirit as they did, and our sainthood will soon be apparent.

JULY 6

SECURE IN GOD

*Whoever listens to me will live in safety
and be at ease, without fear of harm.*

Proverbs 1:33

God's love shines most clearly in the midst of judgment. When the Israelites provoked God by their continued idolatry, He punished them by withholding both dew and rain, but He also took care of His chosen ones.

We may conclude that God's people are safe. If God does not save His people under heaven, He will save them in heaven. So be confident when you hear of wars and rumors of wars. Do not be distressed or agitated. Whatever happens on this earth, you will be secure under the broad wings of Jehovah. Trust in His faithfulness. You can laugh at the bleakest prospects for the future, for it cannot hurt you.

INTERCESSION FOR MINISTERS

Brothers, pray for us.
1 Thessalonians 5:25

Allow me to repeat the apostle's request. Pray for us. Pray for all Christian ministers. Friends, our work is so momentous, involving the well-being of thousands. We conduct an eternal business with people's souls. A very heavy responsibility rests on us.

We want you to profit from our preaching. We want to bring blessing to your children. We want to be useful to both saints and sinners. So dear friends, intercede for us with our God. We will be miserable if your prayers are not backing us up. But we will be very happy if you are supporting us.

Pray then that we may be the "earthen vessels" (2 Cor. 4:7 KJV) into which God may put the treasure of His gospel.

FAITH ASSURED

Tell me the secret of your great strength.
Judges 16:6

What is the secret of the strength of faith? First, faith considers what the promise is. God's promises are emanations of divine grace, overflowings from His great heart.

Then faith asks, "Who gave this promise?" It is God, who cannot lie – God all-powerful, God unchanging. Therefore, faith concludes that the promise must be fulfilled.

Then faith considers the amazing work of Christ as being a clear proof of the Father's intention to fulfill His Word. Faith also looks back to the past. God has never failed us in the past. So faith concludes, "God will not change His ways and leave me now." Faith views each promise in connection with the Promise Giver, and says with assurance, "Surely goodness and love will follow me all the days of my life" (Ps. 23:6).

BLESSED MERCIES

Forget not all his benefits.
Psalm 103:2

Let's look at our own lives. Certainly we will find some incidents that have blessed us and glorified God. Have you had any deliverances? Have you passed through any rivers, supported by God's presence? Have you walked through any fires unharmed? Have you had any moments when God has uniquely revealed His nature to you? Have you had any special blessings?

Surely the goodness of God has been just the same to us as it was to the saints of old. So let us weave His mercies into a song. Let us take the pure gold of thankfulness and the jewels of praise and make them into another crown for Jesus' head.

Let our souls burst forth with music as sweet and as exhilarating as that of David's harp, while we praise the Lord.

JULY 10

CITIZENS OF HEAVEN

Fellow citizens with God's people.
Ephesians 2:19

What does it mean to be a citizen of heaven? It means that we are under heaven's government. Christ the King of heaven reigns in our hearts. We welcome the proclamations issued from the throne of glory. We cheerfully obey the decrees of the Great King.

We share heaven's honors. We share the honors of citizenship, for we have joined the assembly of those whose names are written in heaven. As citizens, we have rights to all the property of heaven. Also, as citizens of heaven, we enjoy its delights. In heaven they rejoice over sinners who repent, prodigals who have returned – and so do we. In heaven they chant the glories of triumphant grace – and so do we. They cast their crowns at Jesus' feet, exult in His smile, and long for His Second Coming. We do, too.

STEADFAST CHARACTER

Christ, after you have suffered a little
while, will himself restore you and
make you strong, firm and steadfast.
1 Peter 5:10

The virtues of Christian character must not resemble the rainbow in its transitory beauty. On the contrary, they must be established, settled, and abiding. Every good quality you possess should be an enduring quality.

May you be rooted and grounded in love (Eph. 3:17).

May your convictions be deep, your love real, and your desires earnest. May your whole life be so firm and steadfast that all the blasts of hell and all the storms of earth will never be able to knock you down. But notice how this steadfastness comes. The Christian is made strong and firmly rooted by all the trials and storms of life. So do not shrink from the rough winds, but take comfort. God is using them to make you firm.

THE WORK OF HOLINESS

Sanctified by God the Father.
Jude 1 KJV

Sanctified in Christ Jesus.
1 Corinthians 1:2

Through the sanctifying work of the Spirit.
1 Peter 1:2

Note the unity of the Three Divine Persons in their gracious acts. In deeds of grace, none of the Persons of the Trinity acts apart from the rest. They are united in their actions as they are in their essence. They are one in their love for us and undivided in the actions that flow from that great love.

See the value that God places on real holiness, since the Three Persons of the Trinity work together to produce a church "without stain or wrinkle or any other blemish" (Eph. 5:27). As a follower of Christ, you should also prize holiness.

HANDLING ANGER

But God said to Jonah,
"Do you have a right to be angry?"
Jonah 4:9

Anger is not necessarily sinful, but it has such a tendency to run wild that, whenever it displays itself, we should be quick to question its character. We should be angry at sin, because of the way it hurts our good and gracious God. We may even be legitimately angry at others, when the sole cause of anger is the evil they do. But it is far more common that our anger is not justifiable.

Does such anger speak well of our Christian faith? Does it glorify God? Many who profess Christianity let their tempers flare as if it were impossible to resist. But our natural tendencies are no excuse for sin.

We must ask the Lord to crucify our tempers and renew us in gentleness and meekness, after His own image.

GOD ALONE

If you make an altar of stones for me,
you will defile it if you use a tool on it.

Exodus 20:25

God's altar was to be built of unhewn stones, so that no trace of human skill or labor would be seen on it. Human wisdom loves to trim and arrange the doctrines of the cross into a system that's more congenial to our fallen nature. We trust in our own ability to approach God. But this is all just an effort to take human tools to God's altar.

We must remember that we cannot perfect the Savior's work. The Lord alone must be exalted in our atonement, and not a single mark of human chisels or hammers will be allowed. Put your tools away and fall on your knees in humble prayer. Let the Lord Jesus be your altar of atonement and rest in Him alone.

PRIVATE PRAYER

The fire must be kept burning on the
altar continuously; it must not go out.

Leviticus 6:13

Keep the altar of private prayer burning. This is the lifeline of holiness. Personal devotion is the very essence, evidence and barometer of vital and experimental religion. Let these times in your "prayer closet" be regular, frequent, and undisturbed.

Are we lukewarm in our private devotions? Is the fire burning dimly in our hearts? God loves to see the hearts of His people glowing. Let us give to God our hearts, all blazing with love. Let us ask Him to keep the fire burning. Many enemies will try to extinguish it, but if God's unseen hand keeps fuelling it, the fire will blaze higher and higher.

Above all, we should be spending time alone with Jesus.

DAILY GRACE

*Each morning everyone gathered
as much as he needed.*

Exodus 16:21

Try to maintain a sense of your entire dependence on the Lord for the things you enjoy each day. Never try to live on the old manna. It all must come from Jesus. Old anointings will not unction your spirit. Your head must have fresh oil poured upon it from the golden horn of the sanctuary. All your comforts lie in His hand.

Our Lord wants us to feel this hourly dependence on Him. He asks us to pray for our "daily bread," and promises, "Your strength will equal your days" (Deut. 33:25). Isn't that best for us, so that we may often go to His throne and be reminded of His love? His rich grace supplies us continually and does not hold back even when we are ungrateful.

CHOSEN BY CHRIST

*For we know, brothers loved by God,
that he has chosen you.*

1 Thessalonians 1:4

Many people want to know, even before they look to Christ, whether they are chosen. But that is something that can only be discovered by "looking unto Jesus."

Look to Jesus and believe on Him. Then you will know you are chosen. For if you believe, you are chosen.

If you give yourself wholly to Christ and trust Him, then you are one of the elect. The assurance of the Holy Spirit will be given to you. Go put your trust in Christ, and His answer will be: "I have loved you with an everlasting love; I have drawn you with loving-kindness" (Jer. 31:3).

There will be no doubt about His having chosen you, when you have chosen Him.

THE REAR GUARD

They will set out last, under their standards.

Numbers 2:31

Cheer up if you feel that you are last and least. Whether you are serving the Lord in a poor village, among untrained peasants, or among the down-and-out on back streets of some city, work on and carry your standards high.

There may be some fiery souls who dash ahead over untrodden paths to learn fresh truth and win more souls to Jesus.

But some, of a more conservative spirit, may legitimately spend their energies reminding the church of her ancient faith and restoring those believers who have strayed. Every position has its duties, and they journey toward the same inheritance.

SEEING GOD'S GLORY

The LORD our God has shown us His glory.
Deuteronomy 5:24

God's great design in all His works is the manifestation of His own glory. Any aim less than that would be unworthy of Him. But how can His glory be revealed to fallen human beings? Our "self" must stand out of the way, so that we may have room to exalt God. This is why He often brings His people into difficult times. When we become aware of our own weakness, we are more prepared to see God's majesty as He comes to deliver us.

The person whose life is smooth and carefree will see little of God's glory, for he has had few moments of self-emptying. So thank God if you have had to travel a rough road. This has allowed you to experience God's greatness and mercy. Your troubles have enriched you with a wealth of knowledge you could not have gained in any other way.

A TASTE OF HEAVEN

A deposit guaranteeing our inheritance.
Ephesians 1:14

What a delightful thing it is to feed on Jesus! Yet our experience of Jesus is imperfect at best – it is only a taste of the goodness He has. We don't yet know how good He is. We only know that His sweetness makes us long for more. We have enjoyed the first fruits of the Spirit, and these have made us hunger and thirst for the fullness of the heavenly crop.

Here we see the manna falling in small bits, there we will eat of the bread of heaven. At present we have many ungratified desires, but soon all our wishes will be satisfied. Anticipate heaven, my friend. Within a short time you will be rid of your troubles. You will share in the triumph of Christ's glory. You will be coheir with the One who is the Heir of all things.

GOD'S ENEMIES

*The Daughter of Jerusalem
tosses her head as you flee.*

Isaiah 37:22

Strong faith enables the servants of God to look with calm contempt on their most haughty foes. We know that our enemies are trying something impossible. They seek to destroy our eternal life. We know their weakness. They are only human. They are utterly powerless to do any damage to the cause of God.

Above all, we know the Most High God is with us. When He puts on His armor, where are His enemies? So put away your fears.

The kingdom is safe in the King's hands. Let us shout for joy, for our God reigns. His enemies cannot win.

A HOLY MARRIAGE

I am your husband.
Jeremiah 3:14

Christ Jesus is joined by His people in a holy marriage. Wooing her by His Spirit, He has brought her to know and love Him. Now He awaits the consummation of their bliss, at the marriage supper of the Lamb.

She has not yet begun to enjoy her exalted position as wife and queen. But on earth, He lovingly performs all the duties of a husband. He provides for her needs, pays her debts, allows her to assume His name and to share His wealth. The love of even the best husband on earth is but a faint picture of the flame that burns in Jesus' heart. His mystical union with the church surpasses any human marriage, for He has left His Father, cleaves to His church, and has become one flesh with her.

SEPARATE FROM THE WORLD

You were like one of them.
Obadiah 1:11

A bad action may be made worse because of the person committing it. When we sin, our offense is especially hurtful. We are the chosen favorites of heaven. We have been forgiven, saved, taught, blessed, and enriched by our Lord.

Do we dare set out to do evil? God forbid! Have you been "like one of them"? At a party, someone starts telling offensive jokes, and everybody laughs, including you – you are like one of them. People complain about money, haggle for bargains, dream about their next major purchase – and you join in. You are like one of them. Could anyone tell the difference?

Be honest with your own soul. Side with the afflicted people of God and not with the world.

FIRM FAITH

*Stand firm and you will see the deliverance
the LORD will bring you today.*
Exodus 14:13

These words contain God's command to the believer in trouble. What do you do when you face terrible trials? The Master says, "Stand firm." Despair whispers, "Give it all up." But God wants us to maintain a cheerful courage, even in our worst times, rejoicing in His love and faithfulness. Restlessness cries, "Do something! Get moving!" But we are not "doing nothing." We are trusting in the Lord who will do everything.

True faith will not listen to presumption, or despair, or cowardice, or restlessness. It only hears God say, "Stand firm." Keep an upright posture, ready for action, expecting further orders, cheerfully and patiently awaiting God's directing voice.

FLEE FROM SIN

*But he left his cloak in her
hand and ran out of the house.*

Genesis 39:12

With certain sins there is no way to win except
by running away. If you want to be safe from
evil acts, hurry away from any opportunity to
do them. Make an agreement with your eyes not
even to look at a tempting sight.

I may be exposed to great danger, so let me
have the serpent's wisdom to stay out of it. It is
better to lose my cloak then to lose my character.
No ties of friendship, no chains of beauty, no
flashes of talent, no arrows of ridicule should
distract me from my wise decision to flee from
sin. When I resist the devil, he will flee from me,
but when I encounter the lusts of the flesh, *I* have
to flee, or else they will win over me.

O God of holiness, preserve Your Josephs.

JEWELS OF CHARACTER

*Make every effort to add to your faith
goodness; and to goodness, knowledge.*

2 Peter 1:5

If you want to enjoy your faith to the fullest, with the Spirit's help: "Make every effort." Make sure that your faith depends on Christ, and Christ alone. Make sure you have goodness. Live boldly with an awareness of what's right. Study the Scripture and get knowledge. Let it dwell in your heart richly.

Add to your knowledge self-control. Have control over both body and soul. Add to this perseverance, that endures hard times. Then pay attention to godliness. Make God's glory the object of your life. Add to that brotherly kindness. Show love to all fellow believers. Then add love, which opens its arms to everyone. When you are adorned with all these jewels, you will be confident of your calling as a Christian.

GOD'S PROMISES

Very great and precious promises.
2 Peter 1:4

If you want to know how precious God's promises are and to enjoy them in your own heart, meditate often upon them. Thinking over these sacred words is often the prelude to their fulfillment. But besides meditating on the promises, try to receive them as the very words of God.

You don't need to concentrate on how great the promise is – that may stagger you – but on how great the promiser is. That will encourage you. Remember it is God – God who cannot lie – who speaks to you. His words are as true as His own existence.

If we meditate on the promises and consider the Promiser, we will ultimately experience their sweetness.

ENVY OF THE WICKED

I was senseless and ignorant;
I was a brute beast before you.

Psalm 73:22

Remember that this is a confession of a man after God's own heart. He has just been describing how he has envied the "arrogant" and begrudged "the prosperity of the wicked." Their problem is that they ignore God. But David finds himself doing the same thing. By envying their success he has forgotten that God is ultimately in control of everyone's destiny.

Are we any better than David? Think back to the times when you have doubted God, when He has proved Himself faithful. You have mistaken His blessings for hindrances. We, too, are senseless and ignorant. But we may also join the psalmist in saying, "You guide me with Your counsel" (v. 24).

I BELONG TO CHRIST

Yet I am always with you.
Psalm 73:23

In spite of all the senselessness and ignorance the psalmist had just been confessing, that did not decrease by one atom the fact that he was saved and accepted, enjoying the blessing of being constantly in God's presence.

Believer, you may enter into this confession and assurance. Try to say, in the same way as the psalmist, "Yet since I belong to Christ, I am always with God." We are always on His mind. He is always thinking about us.

We are before His eyes. He is always watching out for our welfare.

We are always in His hands, so that no one can pluck us out. We are continually on His heart, worn there as a memorial.

THE BITTER HERB OF REPENTANCE

Then Peter remembered ...
And he broke down and wept.
Mark 14:72

JULY 30

Some have suggested that as long as Peter lived, whenever he remembered his denial of Christ, the fountain of his tears began to flow. Many of us who have been redeemed share a similar experience, now that the Spirit has removed our natural hearts of stone.

Can we remain stoic when we remember our sins? We eat our own words with the bitter herb of repentance. When we think of what we promised to be and how different from that we were, we have good reason to weep. The penitent apostle was sure to weep as he recalled the Savior's full forgiveness. To think that we have offended such a kind and gracious Lord – that is enough to make our tears flow.

CHRIST WITH US

I in them.
John 17:23

Consider how deep this union is between our souls and the person of Christ. This is a channel of amazing depth and breadth, along which a great volume of living water may flow. He has set before us an open door. We must not be slow to enter. We are assured of welcome.

He pitches His tent in our humble hearts, so that He may communicate with us constantly. It would be foolish for us not to take advantage of this close communion.

Seek the Lord, for He is near.

Embrace Him; He is your brother.

Hold Him close to your heart, for He is your own flesh and blood.

AUGUST

FIELD OF PROMISES

Let me go to the fields and pick up the leftover grain.
Ruth 2:2

Troubled Christian, come and glean today in the field of promise. There is an abundant supply of precious promises here that will meet your needs. Take this one: "A bruised reed he will not break, and a smoldering wick he will not snuff out" (Is. 42:3). Doesn't that fit your situation?

A reed, helpless, insignificant, and weak. He will not break you. On the contrary, He will restore and strengthen you. Do you want to pick up some more "leftover grain" from the field of Scripture? "Come to me, all you who are weary and burdened, and I will give you rest" (Mt. 11: 28). There is much more to glean. Our Master's field is very rich. Look at all the promises. Gather them up, thresh them out by meditation, and feed on them with joy.

LIVING STONES

Who works out everything in conformity
with the purpose of his will.
Ephesians 1:11

Since we believe God is all-wise, we must believe He has a plan in His work of salvation. What would the creation have been without His design? Is there a fish in the sea, a bird in the air, that was formed by chance?

Since God's hand is apparent in His creation, it is also seen in His grace. He knows the end from the beginning. He sees where each of us belongs. He has not only laid the cornerstone by the blood of His dear Son, but He takes each of us, as stones, out of the quarry, and polishes us by His grace. He has in mind a clear idea of where each stone will be placed.

In the end, it will be clearly seen that God accomplished every part of His great work of grace, according to His purpose, the glory of His name.

HEAVENLY LIGHT

The Lamb is its lamp.
Revelation 21:23

Quietly contemplate the Lamb as the light of heaven. Light in Scripture is a symbol of joy. And this is the joy of heaven: Jesus chose us, loved us, bought us, cleansed us, robed us, kept us, glorified us. We will be in heaven entirely because of Jesus.

Light is also a source of beauty. All the beauty of the saints comes from Jesus. Their lives are beams emanating from the central orb.

Light also symbolizes knowledge. In heaven, our knowledge will be perfect, and the Lord Jesus will be the source of it. When Christ receives His people into heaven, He will touch them with His love and change them into the image of His revealed glory. Whatever light there is, Jesus will be at the center and soul of it.

KNOWING GOD

*The people who know
their God will firmly resist him.*
Daniel 11:32

Every believer understands that knowing God is the best form of knowledge we can have. It is the Spirit's unique task to "lead us into all truth," and all of this is for the advancement of our faith.

Knowledge of God also strengthens our love and strengthens our hope. When we gaze through the telescope of hope, we see the glory that will be revealed, and we anticipate it with joyous confidence.

Knowledge also gives us reasons for patience. There is no Christian virtue that is not advanced by the knowledge of God. That makes it crucial that we grow not only in grace, but also in the "knowledge of our Lord and Savior Jesus Christ" (2 Pet. 3:18).

GOD IS IN CONTROL

*And we know that in all things God works
for the good of those who love him.*
Romans 8:28

There are some things that a believer can be absolutely sure about. We know, for instance, that God is in control. Even when the seas are rough, we know an invisible hand is steering our ship. We know that God is always wise. Knowing this, we are confident that there can be no accidents, no mistakes. Nothing can occur that should not occur.

So believing that God is in control, that He governs wisely, and that He brings good out of evil, we can rest assured able to meet each trial calmly as it comes. The believer can, in the spirit of true submission, pray, "Send me whatever you wish, Lord – as long as it comes from You."

NIGHT WATCHMAN

Watchman, what of the night?
Isaiah 21:11 KJV

What enemies are out there? Sins creep from their lurking places when it is dark. Our heavenly Protector foresees the attacks that are about to come against us. He prays that our faith will not fail. What weather is coming for the church? We need to be concerned about the situation of the church. We need to read the signs of the times. What stars are visible? What precious promises apply to our present situation?

O Watchman, You who sound the alarm, give us comfort, too. And Watchman, when will the morning come? When will the day dawn and the shadows flee away? O Jesus, even if You do not come in person to Your waiting church today, please come in Spirit to my sighing heart and make it sing for joy.

GREAT LOVE

The upright love thee.
Song of Songs 1:4 KJV

Believers love Jesus with a deeper affection than they would dare to give any other being. All their earthly possessions they hold loosely, but they carry Christ close to their hearts. They will gladly deny themselves for His sake, but you can't get them to deny Him. People have tried to separate the faithful from their Master, but in every age these attempts have been fruitless.

This is no everyday attachment that the world's power will eventually dissolve. Yet we constantly lament the fact that we cannot love more. Wouldn't it be wonderful if we could put together all our love, from all believers, in one great collection, and offer it to our great Lord, who is "altogether lovely"?

COBWEBS

They ... spin a spider's web.
Isaiah 59:5

The spider's web is a picture of the hypocrite's religion. How? It's meant to catch his prey. Reputation, praise, and advancement – these are the flies that hypocrites catch in their webs. A spider's web is a marvel of skill. But isn't the hypocrite's religion just as amazing.

A spider's web also comes from within the creature itself. In the same way, hypocrites find their trust and hope within themselves. They forge their own anchor and twist their own ropes. They lay their own foundation and carve the pillars of their own house. They would hate to owe anything to the grace of God.

Cobwebs are not to be tolerated in God's house. Be sure you are resting on something sturdier.

PERFECT BLISS

*The city does not need the sun
or the moon to shine on it.*
Revelation 21:23

The inhabitants of that better world have no need of creature comforts. They need no medicine to cure their diseases. They need no sleep to refresh their bodies, but they tirelessly praise God day and night. They don't need teachers there. The Lord Himself teaches them.

Here we strive for food that perishes and clothes that wear out, but there they find everything in God. What a blessed time that will be, when we finally surpass every secondary blessing and rest on the bare arm of God! What a glorious day, when we will find our joy each day in God and not in His creatures, in the Lord and not in His works. Our souls will have attained perfect bliss.

THE SOURCE OF LIFE

Christ, who is your life.
Colossians 3:4

Paul's marvelously rich expression indicates that Christ is the source of our life. He is also the substance of our spiritual life. It is by His life that we live. He is in us, the hope of glory, the spring of our actions, the central thought that moves every other thought.

Christ is also the sustenance of our life. Christ is the solace of our life. All true joys come from Him. In times of trouble, He is our consolation. Christ is the object of our life. Christ is the model for our life.

If we live in close fellowship with Jesus, we will grow to be like Him. We will walk in His footsteps, until He becomes the crown of our life, in heaven.

RETURN TO INTIMACY

How I long for the months gone by.
Job 29:2

Many Christians view the past with pleasure, but are dissatisfied with the present. There are many possible causes for such a state. It may arise through a neglect of prayer. This is the beginning of all spiritual decline. Or it may be the result of idolatry. Their hearts may be preoccupied with something else, more than with God. The present malaise may also result from self-confidence and self-righteousness. Pride stays busy in our hearts, puffing up our sense of self rather than laying it down at the foot of the cross.

Christian, if you are longing for "the months gone by," don't just wish for a return to the way it was – go to your Master and tell Him about your sorry state. Ask for His grace and strength to help you walk more closely with Him.

DELIGHT IN THE LORD

The LORD reigns, let the earth be glad.
Psalm 97:1

There is no reason to be sad as long as this wonderful sentence is true.

On earth, the Lord's power controls the rage of the wicked just as easily as it controls the rage of the sea. His love refreshes the poor with His mercy just as easily as it refreshes the soil with rain. Majesty gleams in the flashes of lightning in the middle of the storm.

In hell the tormented spirits acknowledge God's supremacy.

In heaven no one doubts the sovereignty of the Eternal King. All fall on their faces to do Him homage. Angels serve Him, the redeemed love Him, all delight to honor Him. May we arrive soon in that city of the great King!

TREES OF GOD

The cedars of Lebanon that he planted.
Psalm 104:16

Lebanon's cedars are symbolic of the Christian. They owe their planting entirely to the Lord. We are not man planted or self-planted but God planted. The mysterious hand of God's Spirit dropped the living seed into a heart that He Himself had prepared. The cedars of Lebanon do not rely on man for their watering. So it is with the Christian who has learned to live by faith. He is independent of other humans, looking to God alone for support.

Like cedars, Christians are full of sap. There is a life force flowing through us, the life of Christ. Finally, the majesty of the cedars is for the glory of God alone. In the believer there is nothing that can magnify man. The Lord has done it all. To Him be all the glory.

HOLY GLADNESS

For you make me glad by your deeds, O LORD.
Psalm 92:4

Do you believe that your sins are forgiven, that Christ has fully atoned for them? Then you should be very happy. With that assurance you can live above the common trial and troubles of the world. Along with your gladness, be grateful and loving. Cling to the cross that took your sin away. Serve the One who served you.

Don't let your love for God evaporate in a few simple choruses of praise. Express your love in strong ways. Love the brothers and sisters of the One who loved you.

Since you have been forgiven freely in Christ, go and tell others the joyful news of God's mercy. Holy gladness and holy boldness will make a good preacher. Cheerful holiness makes a most powerful sermon.

A GOOD THING

He went out to the field one evening to meditate.
Genesis 24:63

Isaac chose a good thing to do. If we were wise, we would spend much time meditating on God's Word – and we would find it interesting. We would all know more, live closer to God, and grow in grace. Isaac chose a good place to do it. We tend to coop ourselves up in little rooms to do our studying. But these are often uninspiring, compared to the outdoors. All of creation points to its Maker, so even the fields can be a holy environment.

Isaac chose a good time to do it. Sunset is appropriate to the kind of meditation that carries us from earthly cares to heavenly communion. The glory of the setting sun delights us, and the oncoming night brings awe. But the Lord is in the city, too. He will meet you in a crowded street or alone in your room. Go to meet Him.

THE GLORY OF GOD

Ascribe to the LORD the glory due His name.
Psalm 29:2

God's glory is the result of His nature and His actions. He is glorious in His character, for He holds within Him everything that is holy, good and lovely.

Glorious actions flow from His character. He loves to reveal His goodness, mercy, and justice to His creatures, but He is also concerned that the glory associated with these actions should be given back to Him and to Him only.

We have nothing in ourselves to boast of, for all that we have we received from God. So we should take care to walk humbly before the Lord. There is room for only one glory receiver in the universe. So the moment we glorify ourselves, we set ourselves up as rivals to the Most High God.

GREAT MERCY

Remember, O LORD, your great mercy.
Psalm 25:6

Meditate a little on the mercy of the Lord. It is tender mercy. With a gentle, loving touch, He heals the brokenhearted and binds up their wounds. It is great mercy. His mercy is like Himself – it is infinite. His mercy is so great that it forgives great sinners for their great sins and then bestows great blessings and great privileges and raises us up to great delights in the great heaven of the great God.

It is undeserved mercy. Deserved mercy is just another name for justice. Our salvation has nothing to do with our merit; God's mercy is the only reason for it. It is rich mercy. It lifts our spirits and soothes our wounds. It is abounding mercy, the supply is not exhausted. It is just as fresh and full and free as ever. It is unfailing mercy. It will never leave you.

STRANGERS AND PRIESTS

Foreigners have entered the
holy places of the LORD's house.
Jeremiah 51:51

This was a shameful thing for the Lord's people. The Holy Place of the temple was reserved for priests alone. We see similar causes for grief nowadays. How many people in our land consider themselves Christians just because they live here? In how many churches do people take communion without any realization of what it means?

We should examine ourselves to see if we belong at the Lord's table. We should make sure that we ourselves are not intruders in the holy place.

The One who struck down the well-meaning Uzzah for touching the ark (2 Sam. 5:6-7) is very protective of His ordinances. Those who approach these ordinances must search their own hearts.

THE SHEPHERD-KING

He will stand and shepherd his flock
in the strength of the LORD.
Micah 5:4

Christ reigns in His church as a shepherd-king. He has the supremacy of a wise and tender shepherd over His needy and loving flock. He commands and receives the willing obedience of well-cared-for sheep, offered joyfully to their beloved Shepherd, whose voice they know so well.

His reign is practical. He is actively involved in providing for His people. His reign is continual. His eyes never sleep. His hands never rest. His heart never stops beating with love. His reign is powerful. The One who stands and cares for the interests of His people is very God of very God. We are fortunate to belong to such a Shepherd, whose humanity interacts with us and whose divinity protects us.

THE SCHOOL OF EXPERIENCE

The sweet psalmist of Israel.
2 Samuel 23:1 KJV

Of all the saints whose lives are recorded in Scripture, David has the most striking, varied, and instructive experiences.

In his story, we find trials and temptations we don't come across elsewhere. David knew the trials of all levels of humanity. This may explain why David's psalms are so universally loved by Christians.

Whatever our frame of mind, whether ecstasy or depression, David has described our emotions perfectly. He is able to instruct our hearts, because he himself was tutored in the best of all schools – the school of heartfelt personal experience. As we are taught in the same school, we appreciate David's psalms more and more.

A Good Measure

He who refreshes others will himself be refreshed.
Proverbs 11:25

This teaches us a great lesson: To get, we must give. To make ourselves happy, we must make others happy. To become spiritually vigorous, we must seek the spiritual good of others. How does this work?

First, our efforts to be useful bring out our own powers of usefulness. We have latent talents that become apparent only when they are used. Also, we find that, in trying to teach others, we learn a great deal ourselves. As we converse with needy saints, we often get a deeper insight into divine truth.

Refreshing others also humbles us. We see how God's grace overshadows our efforts. He grants blessings beyond our expectations, and the people we are trying to help often help us.

HUNGER FOR RIGHTEOUSNESS

O daughters of Jerusalem, I charge you –
if you find my lover, what will you tell him?
Tell him I am faint with love.
Song of Songs 5:8

This is the language of the believer who longs for fellowship with Jesus. He is faint with love. Believing souls are never perfectly at ease unless they are close to Christ.

When they are close to Him, they enjoy the perfect calm of heaven. The closer they are, the fuller their hearts are – full of life, energy, and joy, all coming from Jesus.

If we are not consciously united with Him, it is no wonder that our spirits cry out, "If you find him, tell him I am faint with love!" Behind this desperation, there is a blessing. Jesus said, "Blessed are those who hunger and thirst for righteousness" (Mt. 5:6).

NO MORE CRYING

*The sound of weeping and of crying
will be heard in it no more.*
Isaiah 65:19

Why will there be no weeping in heaven? All external causes of grief will be gone. There will be no pain to distress us, no thought of bereavement or death to sadden us.

We will be perfectly sanctified. No longer will temptations lure us away from the living God. We will stand before His throne, fully conformed to His image. All fear of change will be past. We will know that we are eternally secure.

Eternity will never be exhausted, and our blessedness will go on and on. We will be forever with the Lord. Every desire will be fulfilled. All our faculties will be completely satisfied.

VANQUISHED FOES

*One who breaks open the
way will go up before them.*
Micah 2:13

Because Jesus has gone before us, everything is different. He has conquered every enemy that stood in our way. So cheer up! Not only has Christ traveled the road before you, but He has also defeated your enemies.

Do you dread sin? He has nailed it to the cross. Do you fear death? He has been the death of death. Whatever foes might come up against the Christian, they have all been overcome. Through Christ, God has taken away all the power that is wielded against us. You may go on your journey joyously. Your enemies are vanquished. All you have to do is divide the spoil.

It is true, you will sometimes have to engage in combat – but you will be fighting an already-beaten foe.

TASTING FAITH

His fruit is sweet to my taste.
Song of Songs 2:3

Faith, in Scripture, is spoken of in terms of all the senses. Faith begins with hearing. We hear God's voice, not only with our physical ears, but with our spirits as well. We hear it as God's Word; and we believe that it is from God. Then our minds look at the truth, as it has been presented to us. We perceive its meaning. Then we discover how precious it is; we admire it; we sense its fragrance. That is faith in its "smell".

When we appropriate the mercies of Christ, claiming them for our own, that is touch. Then comes the enjoyment – peace, delight, communion. This is the tasting of faith. To hear Christ's voice as the true voice of God will save us, but the full enjoyment comes when we "taste" Christ, and He becomes food for our souls.

TREASURE OF THE COVENANT

He ordained his covenant forever.
Psalm 111:9

The Lord's people delight in the covenant itself. It is a constant source of comfort as the Holy Spirit leads us to the banquet table, waving a banner of love. We love to contemplate how old the covenant is. Before the daystar knew its place or the planets began to make their rounds, the covenant was already looking out for our interests. Our hearts thrill with joy as we consider how unchanging the covenant is. Neither time nor eternity, life nor death, will ever be able to violate it. We rejoice also in the fullness of the covenant. All things are provided for us. It is also our pleasure to meditate on how gracious the covenant is.

This covenant is a rich treasure chest, a warehouse overflowing with good food, a fountain of life-giving water, a treaty of lasting peace, and a haven of joy.

WEEDS OF DOUBT

How long will they refuse to believe in me?
Numbers 14:11

Work as hard as you can to keep the monster of unbelief away. It is a weed – we can never quite extract its seeds from the soil, but we must keep trying to get at its roots. It is abhorrent. In your case, Christian, it is all the worse. You have received so many mercies from the Lord in the past, how can you doubt Him now?

Jesus has never given us the slightest grounds for suspicion. He has been consistently affectionate and true to us. He has shared His great wealth with us. How can we doubt the all-powerful, all-sufficient Lord? He has more than enough to meet our needs. Countless souls have drawn nourishment from Him, and no one has gone away hungry. So away with this lying traitor, unbelief! He is only trying to cut the tie between us and Christ.

THE OIL OF GOD'S GRACE

Oil for the light.
Exodus 25:6

We all need this oil. Our lamps will not burn long without it. There is no "oil well" within our own natures, so we need to go out and get some.

Only the finest olive oil was to be used in the Lord's service. Similarly, the true believer cannot be satisfied with the fake grace of those who say we are naturally good, or the manufactured grace of religious rituals. No, the Christian goes to the olive press of Gethsemane and draws his supply from the One who was crushed there.

The oil of God's true grace is pure and free from dregs. So our light is clear and bright. Our churches are the Savior's candelabra, and they will require plenty of His grace to shine in this dark world. We should be praying that we might always have a full supply of the oil of God's grace.

INEXHAUSTIBLE MERCY

Have mercy on me, O God.
Psalm 51:1

Even the most experienced and most honored of Christians can only approach God by His free gift of grace. The best men and women seem to be most aware that they are just men and women. Those who merely profess their faith may boast of their spirituality, but the true children of God cry for mercy.

We need the Lord to have mercy on our good works, our prayers, our preachings, our offerings, all our holiest things. If we need mercy for our good works, what can we say about our sins?

It is a great comfort to remember that God's inexhaustible mercy is waiting for us.

WAIT IN FAITH

Wait for the Lord.
Psalm 27:14

Waiting may seem easy, but it takes years to learn. Most of God's soldiers find it easier to march, even double-time, than to stand still. There are times of confusion when the most zealous soul, eagerly wanting to serve the Lord, just does not know what to do.

Wait in prayer. Call on God and spread the case before Him. Wait with a simple heart. When we realize our own inability to choose wisely, we are more willing to be guided by God.

Wait in faith. Keep believing that He will answer you at the right time, whenever that may be.

Wait in quiet patience. Don't complain about your situation, but thank God for it. Accept it as it is and put it all into God's hands, as simply and as wholeheartedly as you can.

IN THE MIDST OF DISTRESS

And wait in hope for my arm.
Isaiah 51:5

In times of severe trial, the Christian has nothing on earth he can trust in, so he is compelled to cast himself on the Lord. We can actually thank God for the hurricanes that blow our souls toward Him.

Since we have only God to trust in, let us put our full confidence in Him. Do not dishonor your Lord by entertaining doubts and fears. Be strong in your faith, giving glory to God. Now is the time for feats of faith and valiant exploits. Be strong and very courageous.

The Lord your God will certainly glorify Himself in your weakness and magnify His might in the midst of your distress.

SEPTEMBER

GOD IS OUR GUIDE

You guide me with your counsel,
and afterward you will take me into glory.
Psalm 73:24

The psalmist felt his need for divine guidance. He had just been discovering the foolishness of his own heart, and to keep himself from being led astray, he decided to let God's wisdom guide him.

A sense of our own ignorance is a good first step toward becoming wise, if it leads us to rely on God's wisdom.

We can be sure that God is our counselor and friend. It is always safe to trust the all-seeing God. He guides us through His written Word. What a great thought this is. God Himself will guide us into glory. We have wandered, strayed, sinned – but He will welcome us home.

Live with this assurance in your heart today.

HEALING PRAYER

Simon's mother-in-law was in bed with a fever, and they told Jesus about her.
Mark 1:30

Household matters are not necessarily a hindrance to one's ministry. In fact, they give us an opportunity to see the Lord's grace at work with our own flesh and blood.

Peter's house was probably a poor fisherman's hut, but the Lord of Glory entered it, lodged there, and worked a miracle.

Is there sickness in your house this morning? Go to Jesus right now and tell Him your problem. We can't be sure that the Lord will immediately remove all disease from those we love, yet prayer is more likely to bring about healing than anything else. Where this does not happen, we must meekly bow to the Lord's will. He is the One who determines life and death.

LOVING JESUS

You whom I love.
Song of Songs 1:7

Can you truly say this about Jesus – "You whom I love"? Many can only say that they hope they love Him, or they think they love Him. But only the shallowest spirituality will stay at this level. Make sure of your love for Jesus, and don't be satisfied until you can speak of your affection for Him as a reality.

True love for God always comes from the Holy Spirit. He may bring it about, but the real reason for loving Jesus lies in Jesus Himself. Why do we love Jesus? Because He first loved us (1 Jn. 4:19). Why do we love Jesus? Because He "gave Himself up for us" (Eph. 5:2). Why do we love Jesus? Because of His excellence. We are filled with a sense of beauty, an awareness of His infinite perfection.

His greatness, goodness, and loveliness combine to enchant our souls.

CLEANSED FROM SIN

"I am willing," he said. "Be clean!"
Mark 1:41

The word of the Lord Jesus has authority. Jesus speaks and it is done. Leprosy yielded to no human remedies, but it went running the moment it heard the Lord's "Be clean!"

The sinner is in a plight worse than the leper. Sinners should follow the lepers example, coming to Christ and begging on their knees, summoning whatever faith they have, to say, "If You are willing, You can make me clean." Is there any doubt what would happen? Jesus heals all who come. He turns no one away. The hand that multiplied the loaves, that saved the sinking Peter, that lifts up troubled saints and crowns believers – that same hand will touch every sinner who seeks Christ and in an instant make him clean.

THIS TROUBLESOME WORLD

Woe to me that I dwell in Meshech,
that I live among the tents of Kedar!
Psalm 120:5

As a Christian, you have to live in the midst of an ungodly world. In Jesus' priestly prayer, He pointedly did not ask His Father to take believers out of this troublesome world (Jn. 17:15).

Remember that people are watching you. Because you are a Christian, they expect more from you than from others. So try to avoid giving anyone an opportunity to find fault with you.

Let your goodness be the only thing "wrong" with you. Try to be useful as well as consistent. The worse the people around you are, the more they need your help. If they are evil, they need you to turn their proud hearts to the truth.

SHINING LIGHTS

In a crooked and depraved generation,
in which you shine like stars in the universe.
Philippians 2:15

We use lights to make things clear. A Christian's life should shine to such an extent that a person could not live with him for a week without knowing the gospel.

Lights are also intended for guidance. We should be pointing sinners to the Savior. We should be ready to explain the meaning of God's Word, the way of salvation, and the Christian life.

Lights also have a very cheering influence. A Christian ought to be a comforter, with kind words on his lips and sympathy in his heart. He should carry sunshine wherever he goes and spread happiness all around.

ACTIVE FAITH

*Since they could not get him to Jesus because
of the crowd, they made an opening in the roof
above Jesus and, after digging through it, lowered
the mat the paralyzed man was lying on.*
Mark 2:4

Faith is full of inventions. The house was full. A crowd blocked the door. But faith found a way of getting to Jesus and bringing the sick man to Him.

If we cannot get sinners to Jesus by ordinary methods, we must use extraordinary ones. When the situation is urgent, we shouldn't mind running some risks and shocking some people's sense of propriety.

When in faith and love we are truly seeking to bring people to Christ, all methods are good and proper.

O Lord, make us quick to invent new ways of reaching those lost in sin, and give us the courage to carry these out, whatever the hazards.

BEARING FRUIT

Your fruitfulness comes from me.
Hosea 14:8

How does this happen? Through our union with Christ. The fruit on the branch of a tree is connected to the roots of that tree. Sever that connection, and the branch dies – no fruit is produced.

Similarly, we bring forth fruit from our union with Christ. Every good work we may do begins in Christ and only comes out in us. Treasure your union with Christ. It is the source of all your fruitfulness. If you weren't joined to Jesus, you would be very barren. We also owe our fruitfulness to God's spiritual providence. For us, it is God's gracious providence that influences us to be fruitful. He is always inspiring, teaching, comforting, strengthening. Without His provision, we would be useless.

THE HIGHER LIFE

*I will answer you and tell you great
and unsearchable things you do not know.*
Jeremiah 33:3

Some parts of the Christian experience are reserved and special. Not all the developments of spiritual life are easy to attain. There are the common feelings of repentance, along with faith, joy, and hope. But there is an upper realm of communion with Christ which goes beyond where most believers are.

There are heights in the things of God that you cannot reach by philosophy or personal brilliance – only God can take us there. But the chariot in which He takes us is made of prayer.

If you want to reach for something higher than everyday experience, look to the Rock that is higher than you (Ps. 61:2), and gaze with the eye of faith through the window of prayer.

FELLOWSHIP WITH JESUS

Jesus went up on a mountainside and called
to him those he wanted, and they came to him.
Mark 3:13

Jesus stands on the mountain, always above the world in terms of holiness, zeal, love, and power. The people He calls must go up the mountain to Him. They must seek to rise to His level by living in constant communion with Him.

Jesus went off by Himself when He wanted close fellowship with His Father, and if we want to be of any service to our fellowmen, we must have that same divine companionship.

This morning, let us climb the mount of communion. There we may be empowered and set apart for our lifework. It is best not to see anyone until we have seen Jesus.

SEPARATE FROM THE WORLD

Be separate.
2 Corinthians 6:17

The Christian is *in* the world but should not be of the world. He should be distinct from the world in terms of his life's goal. To him, "to live is Christ" (Phil. 1:21).

You should also differ from the world in your spirit. Waiting humbly before God, always aware of His presence, enjoying close fellowship with Him, seeking to know His will – in all these ways you will prove you belong to Him.

Your actions should also set you apart. You must avoid wrong for Christ's sake, even if you would benefit from it.

Remember that you are a child of the King of kings. Walk worthy of your heritage.

GOD'S LOVE

The LORD is a jealous God.
Nahum 1:2

Your Lord is very jealous of your love. Didn't He choose you with His own blood? He hates it when you insist that you are your own person or that you can belong to the world. He loved you with such great love that He couldn't stay in heaven without you.

He is very jealous of your trust. God is glad when we lean on Him, and He gets upset when we depend on others or on our own wisdom.

He is also very jealous of our company. He wants us to abide in Him, to stay close to Him. Many of the trials He sends our way are merely to wean our hearts away from the world and toward Him. But His jealousy can also comfort us. For if He loves us this much, He will certainly allow nothing to harm us.

SHOWERS OF BLESSING

As they pass through the Valley of Baca,
they make it a place of springs;
the autumn rains also cover it with pools.
Psalm 84:6

What is the lesson here? When someone finds comfort for himself, the benefits often overflow to others. Interestingly, the pools are filled not by the newly discovered springs, but by the rains. Blessing comes from above rather than below. The pools are useful reservoirs – the pilgrim's labor is not wasted – but it does not supersede God's provision.

Grace can be compared to rain – in its purity, its refreshment, its source (in the heavens), and the will of God that sends it.

I pray that you may have showers of blessing, that the pools dug by others may overflow for you. For what are all our efforts worth unless heaven smiles on us?

SAFE IN A SEA OF TROUBLES

There were also other boats with him.
Mark 4:36

September 14

Jesus was the Admiral of the sea that night. His presence preserved the whole fleet. When we sail in Christ's company, we can't be assured of fair weather. Furious storms rage even around our Lord's vessel, so we shouldn't expect the sea not to toss our little boat. When we go with Jesus, we face the same obstacles He does, but we know we will eventually reach land again.

Jesus is the star of the sea. There may be sorrow on the sea, but when Jesus is there, there is joy, too. May our hearts make Jesus their anchor, their rudder, their lighthouse, their lifeboat, and their harbor. Not a single boat in His convoy will suffer wreck. The Commodore will lead us all safely to port. So whatever squalls may occur, by faith we will be calm.

HANDLING BAD NEWS

He will have no fear of bad news.
Psalm 112:7

Christian, you should not dread the arrival of bad news. If you did not have your God to run to, that would be different. Fear of bad news may lead you into sin. Unbelievers often run toward wrong solutions in their efforts to escape their difficulties. If you begin to be afraid, you may do the same thing.

Trust in the Lord. Wait patiently for Him. If you give way to fear when you hear bad news, then you won't be able to meet the crisis with the composure you need.

How can you glorify God if you play the coward? If you are doubting and despairing, as if there were no hope, how does that magnify the Lord? Take courage. Rely on the faithfulness of God.

THE DIVINE NATURE

You may participate in the divine nature.
2 Peter 1:4

What does this mean? To participate in the divine nature is not to become God. That cannot be. The essence of deity is not participated in. Yet, we, by the renewal of the Holy Spirit, are *re*made in His image – so, we participate in God's nature. "God is love," and we become love. God is truth, and we become true – we love what is true. God is good; and He makes us good by His grace.

We participate in the divine nature in an even higher sense than this. The same life that energized Christ now energizes His people. We are one with Jesus! Remember that those who participate in the divine nature will demonstrate their holy character in their involvement with others, in their daily life.

PRAYING FOR YOUR CHILDREN

Bring the boy to me.
Mark 9:19

In despair, the boy's disappointed father turned from the disciples to Jesus. But the child was delivered from the evil one when his father obeyed Jesus' simple command: "Bring the boy to Me."

Children are a precious gift from God, but a lot of anxiety comes with them. They can bring great joy and great agony to their parents. They may be filled with the Spirit of God or possessed by a spirit of evil. In each case, the Word of God gives the simple answer for curing their ills: "Bring them to Me." We should begin when they are babies, praying earnestly for them. We must never stop praying until they stop breathing.

Whatever this morning's need may be, let it carry you like a swift current to the ocean of God's love.

LIFE AND FAITH

Since we live by the Spirit,
let us keep in step with the Spirit.
Galatians 5:25

The two most important things in our religion are the life of faith and the walk of faith. These are vital points for the Christian. You will never find true faith unaccompanied by true godliness. On the other hand, you will never find a truly holy life that is not rooted in a living faith in Jesus. It is pointless to try to cultivate one without the other.

It doesn't help to build a house without a foundation. Faith and life must go together. Like two abutments of an arch, they will make our piety strong and enduring. O Lord, give us faith within, which comes out in holy lives, glorifying You.

FREE TO RECEIVE

It is for freedom that Christ has set us free.
Galatians 5:1

We are free. We have free access to the Bible. We are free to enjoy the promises of God. Scripture is a treasury always well stocked with grace. It is the bank of heaven. Come in faith, and you are welcome to all the blessings of the covenant. Not a single promise of God's Word will be held back.

In serious trials, this freedom can comfort and cheer you. When sorrow surrounds you, this liberty will soothe you. It is your Father's token of love. Whatever your desires, difficulties, or wants, you may spread it all before Him. It doesn't matter how much you have sinned, you may always ask for pardon and expect to receive it. You are free to enjoy everything that is stored up for you in Christ – wisdom, righteousness, sanctification, and redemption. What a great freedom that is!

BLAZING TORCHES

The sword of the LORD, and of Gideon.
Judges 7:20 KJV

Gideon ordered his men to do two things. They carried torches, but hid them in earthen pitchers. Their first task was to break the pitchers and let the light shine. The second task was to blow the trumpets and shout, "The sword of the Lord, and of Gideon!"

This is precisely what all Christians must do. First, we must shine. Let your good works be such that, when people watch you, they will know that you have been with Jesus. Second, there must be a sound. We must boldly proclaim Christ crucified for sinners. Take the gospel to those who need it. We can do nothing by ourselves, but we can do everything with God's help. So let us determine, in His power, to go out and serve Him, with our blazing torches of holy living and our trumpet tones of bold testimony.

GOD DELIGHTS IN YOU

I will rejoice in doing them good.
Jeremiah 32:41

Why should God take such pleasure in us? We can't delight very much in ourselves, because we often feel burdened. We are sadly aware of our own sin and unfaithfulness. And the rest of God's people can't find much joy in us either. They probably mourn our weaknesses rather than admiring our virtues.

But the Lord rejoices in us. That is exactly what He says to poor, fallen creatures like ourselves, corrupted by sin, but saved, exalted and glorified by His grace. What strong language He uses to express His happiness!

Who would guess that the eternal One would burst forth into song? We should certainly join His song, singing, "I will rejoice in the Lord, I will be joyful in God my Savior" (Hab. 3:18).

REJOICE IN THE LORD

Let Israel rejoice in their Maker.
Psalm 149:2

You have every reason to be glad, my friend, but make sure your gladness has its source in the Lord. You can be glad that the Lord reigns. Rejoice that He sits on the throne. You can sing with the psalmist, "God, my joy and my delight" (Ps. 43:4).

Every attribute of God becomes a fresh ray in the sunlight of our gladness. His wisdom makes us glad; His strength makes us rejoice. Above all, His grace – the overflowing grace of His covenant, the grace that keeps us, makes us holy, perfects us, and brings us to glory – this grace makes us very glad in Him. We should never stop singing, for His new mercies each day should inspire new songs of thanksgiving.

BEING ACCEPTED

Accepted in the beloved.
Ephesians 1:6 KJV

What a privilege! Some days we feel sure that God accepts us because we feel so heavenly minded. But on other days, we fear that we are no longer accepted. If we could only see that the Father's acceptance does not depend at all on our highs and lows, but that we stand accepted on the basis of the One who never changes – how much happier we would be.

You may look at yourself and say, "There is nothing acceptable here!" But look at Christ – there is everything acceptable there. Your sins bother you. But God has put your sins behind His back and accepted you in the Righteous One.

You regularly fight with temptation, but you are accepted in the One who has overcome the powers of evil. Rest assured of your glorious standing in Christ, the beloved.

GOD FIRST

"The gracious hand of our God is on everyone who looks to him, but his great anger is against all who forsake him."
Ezra 8:22

Unfortunately, few believers today feel the kind of holy jealousy for God that Ezra did. Even those who generally walk by faith will occasionally mar the brilliant shine of their lives by asking for human aid where God is sufficient.

It is a wonderful thing to stand upright on the Rock of Ages, upheld by God alone. Would we run so hastily to friends and relatives if we realized how much our Lord is glorified when we rely on Him alone? At times God does use others to help us. But we often begin to trust in them rather than in God. We must learn to honor God by counting on Him first of all.

JUSTIFIED BY FAITH

*Just and the one who justifies
those who have faith in Jesus.*
Romans 3:26

Since we have been justified by faith, we have peace with God. Conscience no longer accuses us. Judgment is now in our favor. Memory looks back on the sins of the past and mourns for them, but has no fear of future punishment. Christ has paid our debt.

God is just. This can be a terrifying thought – unless we also realize that He is a justifier. If God is just, as a sinner I must be punished. But Jesus stands in my place. He takes the punishment for me. Since Jesus has taken our place, bearing the full brunt of divine wrath on our account, we can shout with glorious triumph, "Who will bring any charges against those whom God has chosen?" (Rom. 8:33). My hope, then, rests not in the fact that I am a sinner, but that I am a sinner for whom Christ died.

A PICTURE OF THE CHURCH

Among the myrtle trees in a ravine.
Zechariah 1:8

The church is compared to a grove of myrtle trees flourishing in a small valley. It is hidden, unobserved, secret. The church, like its Lord, has glory, but it is concealed until the time comes to burst forth in radiant splendor.

We also find a hint of tranquil security. Even when opposed and persecuted, the church has a peace that the world cannot give – and cannot take away.

The image of myrtle trees also suggests a picture of constant growth for believers. The church, even in its worst crisis, still has the color of grace. The church prospers most when adversities are most severe. So our text also hints at victory. The myrtle is a symbol of peace and triumph.

RICH IN JOY

Blessed are you, O Israel! Who is like you,
a people saved by the LORD?
Deuteronomy 33:29

Anyone who says Christianity makes people miserable knows nothing about it. That would make no sense. When we become Christians, we enter God's family. And why would God give all the happiness to His enemies and make His own children mourn?

Should the sinner, who has no interest in Christ, be rich in joy, while we go moping like beggars? No, you can rejoice in the Lord always, and glory in your inheritance.

The Spirit is in our hearts, as God's down payment, and He provides substantial benefits even now. But we still look forward to our full inheritance in heaven. Our riches lie beyond the sea. Gleams of glory from that spiritual world cheer us on each day.

GOD CARES FOR YOU

*From heaven the L*ORD
looks down and sees all mankind.
Psalm 33:13

SEPTEMBER 28

There's probably no image that shows God in a better light than when He is depicted stooping from His throne, coming down from heaven to see firsthand the wants and needs of His people. He regularly bends His ear to hear the prayers of dying sinners who long for reconciliation. He pays special attention to us. He marks out our paths; He directs our ways.

We love Him for this. How can we help but pour out our hearts in affection? Your simple sigh can move Yahweh's heart. Your whisper bends His ear. Your prayer of faith can move His arm. No, don't ever think that God sits high and mighty and doesn't care about you. However poor and needy you may be, He is thinking about you.

THE LEPROSY OF SIN

If the disease has covered his whole body,
he shall pronounce that person clean.
Leviticus 13:13

This rule seems strange at first, but there is wisdom in it. If the leper had been completely infected by the disease and still survived, that proved his constitution was basically sound.

We, too, are lepers. When someone sees that he is completely lost, ravaged by sin, when he gives up on all righteous efforts of his own and pleads guilty before the Lord – then he is clean through the blood of Jesus and the grace of God. Hidden, unfelt, unconfessed sin is the true leprosy. But when sin is detected and confessed, it has received its death blow.

Nothing is more deadly than self-righteousness, and nothing heals better than repentance.

CONTINUAL PRAISE

Sing the glory of his name; make his praise glorious!
Psalm 66:2

It is not up to us whether or not we praise God. Praise is due to God, and every Christian, as a recipient of His grace, owes Him thanks daily. It is the Christian's duty to praise God. It is not only a pleasurable exercise, but an absolute obligation. You are bound by the bonds of His love to bless His name as long as you live.

Why do you think He has blessed you? To bless Him back. If you do not praise God, you are not bringing forth the fruit that He, Divine Gardener, has a right to expect from you.

With the dawning of each day, raise a song of thanks, and close each sunset with a hymn. Surround the earth with your praises.

OCTOBER

GIFTS FOR THE LORD

At our door is every delicacy, both new and old,
that I have stored up for you, my lover.
Song of Songs 7:13

The beloved bride wants to give Jesus all she can. Our hearts are filled with "every delicacy, both new and old," stored up for Jesus, the lover of our souls. We have new delicacies. We brim with new life, new joy, and new gratitude.

But we have old delicacies, too. There is our "first love." That is one of our choicest fruits, and Jesus delights in it. There is our first faith – the simple faith that lifted us from a state of utter poverty and allowed us to share in God's great riches. There is that joy we had when we first came to know the Lord.

Whatever blessings or talents or virtues we have, let's give them all to our Beloved. That is when they shine brightest – when Jesus' glory is the solitary aim of our soul.

HEAVENLY HOPE

The hope that is stored up for you in heaven.
Colossians 1:5

Our hope in Christ and the heavenly future He prepares for us keeps us going. It cheers us up to think of heaven, because all that we desire awaits us. That is a land of rest. Fatigue will be banished. In heaven, we will enjoy the victory. The Captain will say, "Well done, good and faithful servant." There we will be perfectly holy. Nothing will creep in to defile that perfect kingdom.

It is sheer joy to realize that we will not be wandering in this wilderness forever, that we will soon inherit the Promised Land. Through God's Spirit, the hope of Heaven can produce great righteousness within us. The person who has this hope inside has a new vigor for his work – for the joy of the Lord is his strength (Neh. 8:10).

MINISTERING ANGELS

*Are not all angels ministering spirits sent
to serve those who will inherit salvation?*
Hebrews 1:14

Angels are the invisible body guards of the saints of God. Loyalty to their Lord leads them to take a deep interest in the children He loves. In biblical times, God's people were sometimes visited by angels. This still happens, though we don't see them. The angels still ascend and descend to visit the heirs of salvation (Gen. 28:12), only now their ladder is Jesus Himself.

Seraphim still fly with burning coals from the altar to touch the lips of the people God chooses (Is. 6:6-7).

If our eyes were opened we would see an army of angels protecting us (2 Kgs. 6:17). Consider the dignity that goes along with this. We are served by the brilliant courtiers of heaven! We are defended by the greatest army ever known!

TWILIGHT TIME

When evening comes, there will be light.
Zechariah 14:7

We often dread the onslaught of old age. We forget that, "when evening comes, there will be light." For many believers, old age is the best time of their lives. Fire no longer flashes from the altar of youth, but the deep glow of earnest feeling remains.

We don't need to dread this time; we can look forward to it. The sun seems larger when it is setting, and it lends a special glory to all the clouds around it.

Even pain does not break the calm of this twilight time, for strength is made perfect in weakness (2 Cor. 12:9).

FOOD FOR STRENGTH

*So he got up and ate and drank. Strengthened by
that food, he traveled forty days and forty nights.*
1 Kings 19:8

God supplies us with great strength when we
need it, but He wants us to use that strength in
His service, not in wanton pleasure seeking or
boasting. We eat the bread of heaven so that we
may be strengthened to serve our Master.

We must move on after we have satisfied
our hunger. Earth should be a preparation for
heaven. Heaven is a place where the saints feast
and work.

Believer, use the strength Christ gives you
to work for Him. We have much more to learn
about His grace. Why does He feed and refresh
our souls? So that we may glorify Him.

THE FOUNTAIN OF LIFE

*Whoever drinks the water
I give him will never thirst.*
John 4:14

The one who believes in Jesus finds enough to satisfy him now and forever. His relationship with Christ is a spring of joy, a fountain of comfort. Shake the foundation of his earthly hopes, but his heart will still be secure, trusting in the Lord. The heart is as insatiable as the grave until Jesus enters it. Then it is a cup that overflows.

The true saint is so completely satisfied with Jesus that he is no longer thirsty – except for another drink from the living fountain. That is the only kind of thirst you should feel, my friend, not a thirst of pain but of love. It is a sweet thing to be panting after a fuller enjoyment of Jesus' love.

TRUE FAITH

*Why have you brought
this trouble on your servant?*
Numbers 11:11

Why does our heavenly Father bring troubles on His servants? To try our faith. If our faith is worth anything, it will stand the test. If you can only trust God when your friends are faithful, your body healthy, and your business profitable, then your faith is poor.

True faith relies on the Lord's faithfulness when friends are gone, when the body is sick, when spirits are depressed, and when it seems that even God is hiding His face.

Our present troubles also serve to heighten our future joy. Isn't peace sweeter after conflict and rest more welcome after a hard day's work? So the memory of our past troubles will enhance our heavenly bliss.

FULL NETS

*Put out into deep water, and
let down the nets for a catch.*
Luke 5:4

This story teaches us, first, the necessity of human effort. The catch of fishes was miraculous, but it still required the use of the fisherman, his boat, and his net. In the saving of souls, the same principle applies. God uses human means. It is certainly His grace alone that saves people, but He still chooses to use the foolishness of preaching.

By themselves, the instruments are ineffective. Christ's presence brings success. When Jesus is "lifted up" in His church, His presence is the church's power. So let us go about our soul fishing today, looking upward in faith and outward in compassion. Let's work hard and trust that the One who goes with us will fill our nets.

ALMIGHTY ARM

Able to keep you from falling.
Jude 24

In a way, the path to heaven is very safe. But in another sense, it is the most dangerous road you could travel. It is beset with difficulties. One false step (and how easy this is to take, if grace is not with us) and down we go.

If our heavenly Father were not holding us up by the arms, we would soon stumble. We also have many enemies trying to push us down. They try to trip us or to throw us over the cliff.

Only an Almighty arm can save us from these invisible foes, who seek to destroy us. We have such an arm enlisted in our defense. He has promised to be faithful. He is more than able to keep us from falling.

FLAWLESS BEAUTY

Before his glorious presence without fault.
Jude 24

Turn around that wonderful phrase in your mind: "without fault." We are far from that now. But our Lord never stops short of perfection in His work of love – and we will reach it someday. All the jewels in the Savior's crown are of the finest quality, without a single flaw.

How will Jesus make us flawless? He will wash us clean from our sins in His own blood, until we are as fair as God's purest angel. Christians will not be out of place in heaven. Our beauty will match the place prepared for us.

What a great day that will be! Sin gone, Satan shut out, and temptation out of the way – and we are presented "without fault" before God!

WHY PRAYER

*Let us lift up our hearts
and our hands to God in heaven.*
Lamentations 3:41

The act of prayer teaches us our own unworthiness. This is a very important lesson for proud beings like us. If God gave us favors without asking us to pray for them, we would never know how poor we were. Through true prayer, we stake our claim on divine wealth, but we also confess our human emptiness. The healthiest state for a Christian is to be always empty of self and constantly dependent on the Lord for supplies – poor in self and rich in Jesus. That is why we pray.

Prayer turns human folly into heavenly wisdom and gives to troubled mortals the peace of God. We thank You, great God, for Your mercy seat. You prove Your marvelous loving-kindness every time You hear our prayers.

THINK ON THESE THINGS

I meditate on your precepts.
Psalm 119:15

Sometimes solitude is better than company, and silence is wiser than speech. We would be better Christians if we spent more time alone, waiting on God, meditating on His Word, gathering spiritual strength to serve Him.

Why should we muse upon the things of God? Because they nourish us. Our souls do not get fed merely by listening to this or that expression of God's truth.

Hearing, reading, studying, and learning – all of these require digestion in order to be truly useful, and digesting truth involves meditation. Many Christians are progressing very slowly in their Christian lives because they do not thoughtfully meditate on God's Word.

TRUE REPENTANCE

Godly sorrow brings repentance.
2 Corinthians 7:10

Genuine spiritual mourning for sin is the work of God's Holy Spirit. Repentance is too precious a flower to grow naturally. Repentance is always the result of God's supernatural grace. If you have even one particle of hatred for sin, God gave it to you.

True repentance always involves Jesus. We must have one eye on our sin and the other on the cross. Better still, we should fix both eyes on Christ and see our sins only in the light of His love.

True sorrow for sin is also very practical. It will make us careful of what we say, and what we do each day. We will take care not to offend or hurt others. Each night we will close the day by confessing our shortcomings, and each morning we will start by asking God to keep us from sinning against Him.

KNOWING JESUS

*I consider everything a loss
compared to the surpassing greatness
of knowing Christ Jesus my Lord.*
Philippians 3:8

Our knowledge of Christ is personal. I cannot rely on anyone else's relationship with Jesus. I must know Him myself. It is an intelligent knowledge. I know Him not as some visionary might dream of Him, but as Scripture shows Him to be. I must know His human nature as well as His divine nature. It is an affectionate knowledge. If I know Him at all, I have to love Him.

Our knowledge of Christ is also satisfying. When I know my Savior, my mind is full to the brim. I have what my soul has been panting after. At the same time, this knowledge is also exciting. The more I know of my Beloved, the more I want to know. So sit at Jesus' feet and get to know Him.

THE DAY OF HIS COMING

But who can endure the day of his coming?
Malachi 3:2

Jesus' first coming was quiet. But even then there were few who passed the test. Those who claimed to be waiting for their Savior showed how shallow their convictions were. They rejected Him when He arrived.

But what will His second advent be like? Can any sinner even stand to think of it? His death shook earth and darkened heaven – what will the day be like when the living Savior summons the living and dead before Him? None of His enemies will be able to withstand the storm of His wrath. Yet His beloved, blood-washed people look forward with joy to His appearing.

Let us examine ourselves and reassure ourselves of our place among His people, so that His coming will not worry us in the least.

THE BREAD OF LIFE

Jesus said to them, "Come and have breakfast."
John 21:12

With these words this morning, you are invited into a holy nearness to Jesus. These words welcome you into His banqueting hall under His redeeming banner of love (Song 2:4). This invitation also speaks of an even closer union with Jesus, because the only food we can feast on when we're with Jesus is Jesus Himself.

This also welcomes us into fellowship with the saints. Even if we cannot all feel the same way, we can all feed the same way, on the bread of life. We also see in these words a source of strength for the Christian. To look at Christ is to live, but for strength to serve Him, we must eat. We must fatten ourselves up, feasting on the gospel, in order to have maximum strength.

OUR FAITHFUL GOD

But David thought to himself, "One of these days I will be destroyed by the hand of Saul."
1 Samuel 27:1

This thought that David had was false. He certainly had no good reason to think that his own anointing was intended as an empty promise. The Lord had never deserted him. He had often been placed in perilous positions, but in every instance God had delivered him.

Don't we doubt God in the same way? Have we ever had the slightest reason to doubt our Father's goodness? Has He ever failed to justify our trust in Him? No! Our God has never left us!

We have had dark nights, but the star of His love shines through the darkness. We may have gone through many trials but they have always resulted in our benefit.

Lord, throw down the Jezebel of our unbelief, and let the dogs devour it.

FELLOWSHIP AND PRAYER

Your carts overflow with abundance.
Psalm 65:11

What are these "carts" that overflow with good things for us? One special one is certainly the cart of prayer. If a believer frequents the prayer closet, he or she will never lack spiritual nourishment.

When you wrestle with God in prayer, you grow strong – even if the wrestling is sometimes difficult. But there's another cart that overflows with nourishment for the Christian – the cart of communion. How delightful it is to have fellowship with Jesus! Earth has no words to describe this holy sense of calm. There are even few Christians who understand it. They spend all their time in the valleys and seldom climb the mountain. Don't make that mistake, dear reader. Sit under the shadow of Jesus. Enjoy His presence and you will be greatly satisfied.

HEIR OF ALL THINGS

Mere infants in Christ.
1 Corinthians 3:1

Do you feel that your spiritual life is weak? Does it bother you that your faith is small, your love feeble? Cheer up. You still have reason to be thankful. Remember that in some things you are equal to the most experienced, most full-grown Christian.

You are bought with the blood of Christ, just as much as the greatest saint is. You are just as much an adopted child of God. You are just as completely justified, because justification doesn't happen in degrees.

Even your small faith has made you thoroughly clean. You have just as much right to the promises in the covenant itself. You may be poor in faith, but in Jesus you are the heir of all things.

GROWING IN GRACE

In all things grow up into him.
Ephesians 4:15

Many Christians have stunted their growth in spiritual things. Every year, they're the same. There's no advance, no upspringing. They exist but they don't grow.

Should we be satisfied just believing in Christ and not longing to move more and more into His fullness? No! As good traders in heaven's market, we should keep trying to gain more of the knowledge of our Lord.

To ripen in grace, we must live close to Jesus, in His presence, ripened by the sunshine of His smiles. Then we will find ourselves advancing in holiness, in love, in faith, in hope – in every precious gift.

ACTS OF LOVE

For Christ's love compels us.
2 Corinthians 5:14

How much do you owe the Lord? Has He ever done anything for you? Has He forgiven your sins? Has He written your name in His book of life? Then do something for Jesus that is worthy of His love.

How will you feel when your Master shows up and you have to confess that you did nothing for Him? Think of how He has loved you and given Himself for you. Do you know the power of that love? Then let it be like a powerful wind sweeping through your soul, blowing away the clouds of worldliness and the mists of sin.

Fix your heart on God with a steadfast confidence, and honor Him with acts of heartfelt devotion.

FREE GRACE

I will love them freely.
Hosea 14:4

This simple sentence is a powerful theology lesson. It encapsulates the glorious message of salvation that was given to us by Jesus Christ our Redeemer. The sense of this verse hinges on the word "freely." This is the glorious way that love streams from heaven to earth, a spontaneous love flowing forth to those who don't deserve it, can't afford it, and don't seek it. It is, in fact, the only way God can love us, considering how sinful we are. If there were any way that we earned His love, that would diminish the freeness of it. Remember, there are no conditions to the covenant of grace. We can set foot on the promise of God and stand secure.

Isn't it great to know that God's grace is utterly free to us?

NO ONE LIKE JESUS

You do not want to leave too, do you?
John 6:67

Many have forsaken Christ and have stopped walking with Him. But what reason could you have to make such a change? When you have simply trusted Jesus, have you ever been let down? Haven't you always found Jesus to be a compassionate and generous friend? We have the joy of salvation – why give that up? Who trades gold for mud?

We will never give up the sun until we find a better light, and we'll never leave our Lord until a brighter lover appears. And that will never happen.

When this world is especially troubling, we find it very relaxing to rest upon our Savior. We say with Peter, "Lord, to whom shall we go?" (Jn. 6:68).

WELL-WATERED TREES

The trees of the LORD are well watered.
Psalm 104:16

Without water, the tree cannot flourish – or even exist. In the same way, vitality is essential to a Christian. There must be life – the vital force infused into us by God's Holy Spirit. It is not enough to bear the name Christian: We must be filled with the spirit of divine life.

Consider how constantly active the moisture is within the tree. Similarly, the Christian life is full of energy, not always bearing fruit, but often in inner growth. The believer's character is always developing, becoming more like Christ. With the tree, the water eventually produces fruit. So it is with a truly healthy Christian. The work of the Spirit can be seen in how he walks and talks. There is so much life-giving Spirit within, that his whole being vibrates with divine power.

THE STRENGTH OF TRUTH

*Because of the truth, which lives
in us and will be with us forever.*
2 John 2

Once the truth of God enters the human heart and gets control of a person, nothing can dislodge it. We entertain it not as a guest, but as the master of our house. This is an essential part of the gospel. Those who know the power of the Holy Spirit – opening the Word, applying it to our lives and sealing it there – would rather be torn in pieces than to be torn away from the gospel.

A thousand mercies are wrapped up in this assurance: The truth will be with us forever. It will be our support as long as we live and our comfort as we die. It will be a song in our hearts and our glory through all eternity.

As our love for God's truth grows, we grow in love as well. Our compassion goes beyond boundaries.

GENEROUS GIVING

Because of my house, which remains a ruin,
while each of you is busy with his own house.
Haggai 1:9

Stingy people cut back their contributions to church ministry and missionary support and they call such saving "good economy." They forget that neglecting the house of God is a sure way to bring ruin on their own houses.

Scripture teaches that the Lord enriches the one who gives freely and allows the miser to discover the sad result of his penny-pinching. I have noticed that the most generous Christians have always been the happiest.

Selfishness looks first to its own house, but godliness seeks first the kingdom of God and His righteousness (Mt. 6:33). It takes faith to be so generous, but surely the Lord deserves it.

TRUSTWORTHY SAYINGS

Here is a trustworthy saying.
2 Timothy 2:11

Paul has four of these "trustworthy sayings." The first is: "Christ Jesus came into the world to save sinners" (1 Tim. 1:15). The next is "godliness has value for all things" (1 Tim. 4:8). The third – "if we endure we will also reign with him" (2 Tim. 2:12). And the fourth – "having been justified by his grace, we might become heirs having the hope of eternal life" (Tit. 3:7).

We may trace a connection between these sayings. The first lays the foundation of our eternal salvation. The next affirms the double blessing we get through this salvation. The third shows our duties toward God. The last one sends us off into Christian service.

Treasure these trustworthy sayings. Let them guide your life, comfort you and teach you.

CHOSEN BY GOD

I have chosen you out of the world.
John 15:19

Those who doubt the doctrines of grace or prefer not to consider them are missing the choicest clusters of God's vineyard. This is honey that brightens the heart – to love and learn the mysteries of God's kingdom. Seek to enlarge your mind, so that you can comprehend more and more of the eternal love of God.

Consider this: If Jesus Himself promises to bring you to glory, and if the Father Himself promised to give you to the Son as part of His infinite reward, what can happen to you? Unless God Himself is unfaithful, or unless Jesus goes back on His promise, you are utterly safe. So come, exult before the God of grace and leap with joy – because He has chosen you.

HOW TO PRAY

This, then, is how you should pray:
"Our Father in heaven."
Matthew 6:9

This prayer begins where all true prayer starts, with the spirit of adoption: "Our Father." But then the childlike soul begins to understand the grandeur of the Father and ascends into heartfelt adoration. There is only a small step from adoring worship to a glowing missionary spirit: "Your kingdom come, Your will be done."

Next follows an expression of dependence on God: "Give us this day ... " As you are illuminated by the Spirit, you realize that you are sinful, so you beg for mercy: "Forgive us ..." Then knowing you are accepted by God, you ask for strength. Finally, a result of all this, there is triumphant praise: "for Yours is the ... glory forever."

THE POWER OF PRAISE

I will praise you, O LORD.
Psalm 9:1

Praise should always follow answered prayer. Has the Lord been gracious to you? Then praise Him as long as you live. To be silent over God's mercies is to be guilty of ingratitude. To forget to praise God is to neglect a great benefit for ourselves.

Praise, like prayer, is one great way to develop our own spiritual life. It removes our burdens, excites our hope, increases our faith. It is an invigorating exercise that quickens our pulse and prepares us for new ways of serving God. Blessing God for the mercies we have received can also benefit those around us.

Praise is the most heavenly of Christian duties.

REPENTANCE

Renew a steadfast spirit within me.
Psalm 51:10

When a backslider is restored, the experience is similar to the original conversion. Repentance is required. We needed God's grace to come to Christ at first, and we need it to come back to Him. No one can experience this renewal without the same burst of the Holy Spirit's energy that he felt at his conversion.

If you feel weak, my friend, let your weakness lead you to pray for help. Plead with God for a new spirit.

Prayer is the method God uses to achieve His results. So pray often. Dwell on God's Word. Guard against future uprisings of sin. Keep doing the things that nourish your spiritual life and keep praying David's prayer.

NOVEMBER

HOME CHURCH

The church that meets in your home.
Philemon 2

Is there a "church" in your home? Is there someone from your household or friend of the family who needs to know Christ? Pray especially for that person this morning, that he or she would "return home," refreshing the hearts of all the saints (Phlm. 7). And if there is a "church" in your home, make sure it is well-ordered.

We should all be moving through our activities with holiness, diligence, kindness, and integrity. You see, more is expected of a church than a mere household. Family worship must be more devout and exciting. Love within the home must be warm and unbroken. And our external conduct must be more Christlike. Let's trust Christ to give us grace to shine before others with glory.

GOD DOES NOT CHANGE

I the LORD do not change.
Malachi 3:6

Despite all the changes in the world around us, there is One who never changes. Life is variable in every aspect, it seems, but there is One whose heart is fixed. This is the stability that an anchor gives a ship. It is the basis for Christian hope.

God "does not change like shifting shadows" (Jas. 1:17). Whatever His character has been in the past, it still is now. His power, His wisdom, His justice, and His truth – all are unchanged. He has always been a refuge for His people, their stronghold in the day of trouble, and He will continue to be their strong helper. And His love never changes. He loves us now as much as He ever did. This gives us precious assurance.

COMFORT IN PRAYER

For he is praying.
Acts 9:11

NOVEMBER 3

Prayers are instantly noticed in heaven. Here is comfort for the distressed (but praying) soul. Often a brokenhearted person will get on his knees but can only utter his plea in the language of sighs and tears. Yet that groan makes all the harps of heaven vibrate with music. The tear is caught by God and treasured.

Do not think that your prayer, even weak and trembling, will go unnoticed. Not only does God hear our prayers, but He loves to hear them. "He does not ignore the cry of the afflicted" (Ps. 9:12). Wherever there is a heart bursting with sorrow or a lip quivering with pain or a deep groan or a repentant sigh – then the heart of Yahweh is open.

IN GOD'S STRENGTH

My power is made perfect in weakness.
2 Corinthians 12:9

A primary qualification for success in serving God is a sense of our own weakness. Those who serve God must serve Him in God's way, in God's strength, or He will not accept their service. Whatever man does without God's help, God can never claim as His own. He wants only the grain that grows from the seed sown from heaven, watered by grace and ripened by the sun of His divine love.

God will empty out everything that's in you before He fills you with Himself.

Are you bothered by your own weakness? Take courage, because there must be an awareness of weakness before the Lord gives you victory. Your emptiness is just the preparation for being filled.

VICTORIOUS IN CHRIST

No weapon formed against you will prevail.
Isaiah 54:17

November 5

The history of the church is full of examples of weapons forged against God's people. At first, the early Christians in Judea had to withstand opposition from their fellow Jews. Then, for about 250 years, the Roman Empire had Christians arrested, tortured, and killed in savage ways. But even these horrendous methods did not prevail against Christ's church.

"Take heart!" Jesus said. "I have overcome the world" (Jn. 16:33). New weapons were forged, weapons of false teaching. But those weapons have not prevailed either. God's truth goes on. Let us praise the Lord today that He has delivered His people from the many weapons forged against them.

DRENCHED BY GRACE

For I will pour water on the thirsty land.
Isaiah 44:3

Are you thirsting this morning for the living God? Are you depressed because the delight of God is missing from your heart? Are you becoming aware that you are barren, like the dry ground, that you are not bringing forth the fruit God expects of you? Then here is exactly the promise you need. You will receive the grace you need; you will have plenty.

As water refreshes the thirsty, so grace will gratify your desires.

As water awakens the sleeping plants, so a fresh supply of grace will awaken you.

As water swells the buds and makes fruit ripen, so will you become fruitful in the ways of God. You will be drenched by grace.

IN HIS HANDS

*See, I have engraved you
on the palms of my hands.*
Isaiah 49:16

Look for yourselves! Here is the truth! We are engraved on His hands! All creation may marvel that we are given such a precious place. And note: He doesn't say He has engraved our names, but us, on the palms of His hands.

Think of it! He has engraved your image, your circumstances, your sins, your temptations, your weaknesses, your wants, and your works – everything about you is on His hands. How could you ever think He has forgotten you?

RECEIVING CHRIST

As you received Jesus Christ as Lord.
Colossians 2:6

The life of faith is a receiving. This implies the very opposite of any idea that we could earn our salvation. It is just the accepting of a gift. We are empty vessels into which God pours His salvation. The idea of receiving implies a sense of realization, that is, making the matter a reality. As long as we are without faith, Jesus is a mere name to us. But by an act of faith Jesus becomes a real person in our consciousness. But receiving also means getting possession of. The thing I receive becomes my own. When I receive Jesus, He becomes my Savior, so much mine that neither life nor death can rob me of Him.

We have received Christ Jesus Himself. It is true that He has given us much – life, pardon, and righteousness. These are all precious, but we have even more – Christ Himself.

WALK IN CHRIST

Continue to live in him.
Colossians 2:6

If we have received Christ into our innermost hearts, our new life will demonstrate our intimate acquaintance with Him. The word for "life" in this verse is the word for "walk." The apostle pictured us walking through life in Jesus. If a person "walks" in Christ, he acts as Christ would act. Since Christ is in him, he will bear the image of Jesus.

Walking signifies progress. Keep moving forward until you reach the ultimate level of the knowledge of our beloved Lord. Walking also has to do with habit. Christ must fill us to the point that He affects our instincts and He changes our habits. We must live and move and have our being in Him. Yes, we received Christ as Lord – He entered our lives through no merit of our own. But now we must "walk" in Him.

AT HOME WITH GOD

The eternal God is your refuge.
Deuteronomy 33:27

The word "refuge" may also be translated "mansion" or "home," which yields a new thought. God is our home. Home is precious, even if it's a humble cottage. Yet God is even more dear to us than that.

At home we feel safe. In the same way, God is our shelter and retreat. At home we rest. So our hearts find rest with God after we get tired of life's conflicts. At home, we express ourselves freely. Similarly, we can communicate with God, speaking of all our hidden desires.

Home is also the place of our greatest happiness. And in God we find our deepest delight. Our joy in the Lord surpasses all other joys.

SAFE IN HIS ARMS

November 11

Underneath are the everlasting arms.
Deuteronomy 33:27

God – the eternal God – is our support at all times, especially when we are sinking in some deep trouble or concern. Sometimes a Christian sinks low in shame and humility. He has such a deep sense of his own sinfulness that he hardly knows how to pray. Sin may drag you down, but Christ's atonement still supports you.

On some occasions, a Christian will be sinking from an external trial. Every earthly support has been cut away. What then? Underneath are still the "everlasting arms." You cannot fall so far that God's gracious arms cannot reach you. You may even be sinking under internal struggles, but the everlasting arms are still embracing you. This assurance of support is a great comfort to those who are working hard in God's service.

FAITH IN TRIALS

So that your faith may be proved genuine.
1 Peter 1:7

If faith is not tested, it may be true faith, but it will certainly be small faith. It will probably remain undersized until it is tested. Faith prospers most when things go against it. Storms are its teachers, and lightning just reveals its truths. No faith is as precious as faith that triumphs through adversity. Tested faith brings experience.

How else will you learn your own weakness and the power of God to help you, unless you have to rely on His support to pass through the raging rivers?

You don't have to seek trials; they will come to you. But even if you can't claim the benefits of a lengthy experience of tested faith, thank God for the grace He gives you now.

BEARING FRUIT

No branch can bear fruit by itself.
John 15:4

How did you begin to bear fruit? It was when you came to Jesus, threw yourself on His great atonement, and rested on His righteousness. Have you declined since then? Discover those activities that have drawn you closest to Christ, and spend time doing them.

If you want to bear fruit, you have to stay close to Him. So any activity that gets you close to Him will help you bear fruit.

Consider your own life. Where have you lacked fruit? Some of us have to learn the hard way that all good things come from Christ. We reach a point of utter barrenness in our own lives before we realize how weak we really are. Then we simply depend again on the grace of God; we wait on the Holy Spirit; and the fruit returns.

ONE GOD

I will cut off from this place those who
bow down and swear by the LORD
and who also swear by Molech.
Zephaniah 1:4-5

These people thought they were safe because they
belonged to both parties. They worshiped with
the followers of Yahweh, and they also bowed to
Molech. But God hates such duplicity. He can't
stand hypocrisy.

My friend, search your own soul this morning.
See whether you are guilty of double-dealing.
You profess to be a follower of Jesus – do you
really love Him? Is your heart right with God?
To have one foot on the land of truth and another
on the sea of falsehood will lead to a major fall
and ruin.

Christ will be all or nothing. God fills the
whole universe, so there is no room left for any
other god. If He reigns in your heart, there will
be no space left for another master.

THE LORD'S PEOPLE

For the Lord's portion is his people.
Deuteronomy 32:9

God's people are not only His by choice, but also by purpose. He has bought and paid for them, so there can be no disputing His claim. He bought them not with perishable things like silver and gold, but with the precious blood of Jesus (1 Pet. 1:18-19).

The price has been paid in open court and the church belongs to the Lord forever. He doesn't forget anyone He has redeemed. He counts all the sheep for whom He lays down His life. We are the conquered captives of His omnipotent love. We have been chosen, bought and won, and the Lord's rights to us are incontestable. So let us live each day to do His will and to show forth His glory.

THE SOUL'S INHERITANCE

I say to myself, "The LORD is my portion."
Lamentations 3:24

It is not, "The Lord is partly my portion." No, He makes up the sum total of my soul's inheritance. Within the circumference of that circle lies everything we possess or desire.

The Lord is my portion. Not only His grace or His love or His covenant, but Yahweh Himself. God is complete in Himself.

If He is all-sufficient for Himself, He must be all-sufficient for us. We delight in the Lord, who lets us drink freely from the river of His pleasures.

Let us rejoice in Him, showing the world how much God has blessed us.

GIVING GOD GLORY

To him be the glory forever! Amen.
Romans 11:36

This should be the greatest desire of any Christian. All other wishes must give way to this one. The Christian may want to improve his character, but only for the purpose of giving God glory. You should not be driven by any other motivation. Don't let anything make your heart beat as strongly as your love for God does.

Let God be your sole delight. Your desire for God's glory should be a growing desire. If God has enriched you with experience, then praise Him with a stronger faith than you had at first. Have you gained knowledge over the years? Then you can sing His praises more sweetly. If you have enjoyed happy times, then let your music swell with glory for God.

THE HEART OF THE BELIEVER

A spring enclosed, a sealed fountain.
Song of Songs 4:12

This metaphor can apply to the inner life of the believer. First, we find the idea of secrecy. It is a spring enclosed. In biblical times there were springs that buildings constructed over them, so that no one could get to them except those who knew the secret entrance. So is the heart of the believer, when it has been renewed by God's grace. There is a mysterious life within that no other human can touch.

Today's text speaks also of separation. This is not the community spring. It is set apart from the others. It bears a unique mark, a king's royal seal.

We also find a sense of sacredness. The spring is preserved for the use of some special person, just like the Christian's heart.

WISE AND FOOLISH QUESTIONS

But avoid foolish controversies.
Titus 3:9

It is better to spend our time doing good than arguing about things that are, at best, of minor importance. Our churches have suffered greatly from petty battles over obscure points and trivial questions. Wise believers avoid questions on points where Scripture is silent, on mysteries that belong to God alone, on prophecies of doubtful interpretation, and on methods of observing human rituals. We must follow the apostle's advice and devote ourselves to doing what is good (v. 8).

There are, however, some questions that are the opposite of foolish: Do I believe in the Lord Jesus Christ? Am I renewed in the spirit of my mind? Am I growing in grace? What more can I do for Jesus?

A GRATEFUL SPIRIT

O LORD, you took up my case.
Lamentations 3:58

Notice how positively the prophet speaks. He does not say, "I hope, I trust, I sometimes think, that God has taken up my case." No, he speaks of it as something that cannot be disputed.

In the same way, we must shake off our doubts and fears. See how gratefully the prophet speaks, giving all the glory to God alone. He doesn't credit any human effort with his redemption. No, it's, "You took up my case; You redeemed my life." We should always cultivate a grateful spirit.

Children of God, seek to have a vital experience of the Lord's mercy. When you have it, speak positively of it, sing gratefully, and shout triumphantly.

THE LIFE OF THE SPIRIT

And do not grieve the Holy Spirit.
Ephesians 4:30

All the believer has must come from Christ, but it comes only through the channel of the Holy Spirit. Just as all blessings come to you through the Spirit, so all good things that come from you are a result of the Spirit's sanctifying work in your life. No holy thought, devout worship, or grace-filled act can happen apart from the Spirit in you.

Child of God, you have no life in you apart from the life God gives through His Spirit. So do not grieve the Spirit or make Him angry by sinning against Him. Do not quench the Spirit by ignoring His whispers in your soul. Be ready to obey every suggestion He offers. We must realize how weak we are without Him and then depend entirely on His strength.

TENDING SHEEP

Israel served to get a wife,
and to pay for her he tended sheep.
Hosea 12:12

Jacob, arguing with Laban, described how hard he had worked. Our Savior's life on earth was even more difficult. He watched over all His sheep: "I have not lost one of those you gave me" (Jn. 18:9). And sleep fled from His eyes as He wrestled in prayer all night for His people. If Jesus had chosen to complain, He could have moaned louder than any underappreciated shepherd. Like Jacob, He did it in order to win His bride.

We can go further with this spiritual parallel. Laban required Jacob to account for all the sheep. If any were killed by beasts, Jacob had to make up for it. Wasn't Jesus in a similar position? He was under obligation to bring every believer safely into the Father's hand – even if it meant His death.

FELLOWSHIP WITH CHRIST

Fellowship with him.
1 John 1:6

November 23

When we were united to Christ by faith, we were brought into fellowship with Him. His interests and ours became mutual.

We have fellowship with Christ in His love. What He loves, we love. We have fellowship with Him in His desires. He desires God's glory – and we work toward the same goal. He wants His Father's name to be loved and adored by all His creatures.

We also have fellowship with Christ in His suffering. We are not nailed to a cross, but we share the burden of prejudice that people have against Him. We also share Christ's work, ministering to people with words of truth and deeds of love. We share Christ's joys. We are happy when He is happy. Finally, His glory will complete our fellowship.

Abundance from the Lord

There the Lord will be our Mighty One.
It will be like a place of broad rivers and streams.
Isaiah 33:21

Broad rivers and streams produce fertile ground and abundant crops. That is what God does for His church. With God, the church has abundance. Is there anything the church could ask for that the Lord would not give her? He promises to supply all our needs.

Do you crave the bread of life? It drops like manna from the sky. Do you thirst for refreshing streams? The rock that brings forth water is right in front of you – that Rock is Christ. If you are in need, it is your own fault.

Broad rivers and streams especially denote security. In ancient days, rivers were a defense. What a defense the Lord is for His church! Satan may try to invade, but he cannot cross this broad river of God.

TRUE FREEDOM

To proclaim freedom for the prisoners.
Luke 4:18

No one but Jesus can offer freedom to prisoners. True freedom comes only from Him. It is a freedom righteously granted. The Son, heir of all things, has the right to make people free.

Our salvation occurs within the perfect justice of God. Our freedom has been expensive to purchase. Christ proclaims freedom with His powerful word, but He bought it with His blood. We go free because He took our punishment. We have liberty because He faced suffering in our place. But although it has been costly, our freedom is freely given. Jesus asks nothing from us. He saves us just as we are, without any merit on our part. When Jesus sets us free, our freedom is eternally secure. Let our freedom be practically demonstrated as we serve God in our daily lives with gratitude and delight.

SERVE GOD TODAY

Whatever your hand finds to do,
do it with all your might.
Ecclesiastes 9:10

This refers to actions that are possible. There are many things that our hearts want to do that will never come about. That is fine, but if we want to be truly effective, we should not be content with talking about the schemes of our hearts. No, we must practically carry out "whatever our hands find to do."

One good deed is worth more than a thousand brilliant theories. We should not be waiting for great opportunities or for a different kind of work, but we should just do the things we "find to do" each day. Don't wait until your Christian experience has ripened into maturity – serve God now. No one ever served God by doing things "tomorrow." We honor Christ by what we do today.

SERVE THE LORD IN HOLINESS

*Joshua the high priest standing
before the angel of the LORD.*
Zechariah 3:1

In Joshua the high priest, we see a picture of every child of God who has been brought to God by the blood of Christ and taught to serve the Lord in holiness. Jesus has made us priests and kings unto God, and even here on earth we exercise the priesthood of holy living and devoted service. But this high priest is described as "standing before the angel of the Lord," that is, standing to minister.

This should be the position of every true believer. Every place is God's temple, and we can serve Him just as well in our daily lives as in His house. We should always be ministering, offering the spiritual sacrifice of prayer and praise, and presenting ourselves as "living sacrifices."

WALK IN THE TRUTH

*It gave me great joy to have some brothers come
and tell about your faithfulness to the truth
and how you continue to walk in the truth.*
3 John 3

The truth was in Gaius, and Gaius was in the
truth. If that first statement were not the case,
the second would not be true either. Truth must
enter a soul, penetrate it, and saturate it, or else it
does no good. Once your heart begins to digest
the true doctrine, it can sustain you and build
you up.

Truth must be a living force within us, an
active energy, an indwelling reality. If it is in
us, then we cannot do without it.

When the truth is kindled within us, its
brightness soon beams forth in our eternal life
and conversation. Walking in the truth involves
a life of integrity, holiness, faithfulness, and
simplicity – the natural products of the gospel
of truth.

DO NOT SLANDER

Do not go about spreading
slander among your people.
Leviticus 19:16

NOVEMBER 29

Slander contains a triple-action poison. It harms the teller, the hearer, and the person who is slandered. Whether the report is true or false, God's Word tells us not to spread it.

The reputation of the Lord's people should be very precious in our sight. Many people take a special delight in tearing down their fellow Christians, as if they were raising themselves up in the process.

One of these days, you may need understanding and silence from others, so give it cheerfully to those who need it now. This should be our general rule: "to slander no one, to be peaceable and considerate, and to show true humility toward all men" (Tit. 3:2).

GOD WILL PROVIDE

Amaziah asked the man of God, "But what about the hundred talents I paid for these Israelite troops?" The man of God replied, "The LORD can give you much more than that."
2 Chronicles 25:9

This seemed to be a very important matter to King Amaziah. Maybe you can understand that. Losing money is never pleasant, and even when it is a matter of principle, we often find ourselves unwilling to make that sacrifice. When it's a matter of survival, the need for money can outweigh other doctrines. But our Father holds the purse strings. What we lose for His sake He can repay a thousand times over.

We must merely obey His will, and we can be sure that He will provide for us.

The Lord has bequeathed this earth to the meek, and He will not withhold any good thing from those who live according to His principles (Ps. 84:11).

DECEMBER

THE WINTER OF THE SOUL

You have made both summer and winter.
Psalm 74:17

If God is true to His Word in the revolving of the seasons, He will certainly prove faithful in His dealings with His own beloved Son. The winter of the soul is not a comfortable season at all. But this may comfort you: The Lord has made it. He sends the sharp blasts of adversity to nip the buds of expectation. They come to us by His wise design.

Frost breaks up the earth and enriches the soil. In the same way, good things can result from our winters of affliction.

Our Lord is a constant source of warmth and comfort in our times of trouble. Let's wrap ourselves in the warm sweaters of His promises and then go out into the cold and continue our service for Him.

JESUS LOVES THE CHURCH

All beautiful you are, my darling.
Song of Songs 4:7

The Lord's admiration for His church is wonderful. He describes her beauty in glowing terms. She is not merely "beautiful," but "all beautiful." He sees her in Himself, washed in His atoning blood and clothed in His righteousness. Holiness, glory, excellence – these are His robes that His lovely bride is wearing. Through her Lord she has gained a position of righteousness – and that makes her beautiful to behold. Her excellence and worth cannot be rivaled by all the nobility and royalty of the world.

Jesus has written it in His Word and He sounds it forth even now. One day, from His glorious throne, He will confirm it. "Come, you who are blessed by my Father," He will say (Mt. 25:34).

FREE FROM DEFECT

There is no flaw in you.
Song of Songs 4:7

The Lord has just announced how beautiful His church is. Now He adds a precious negative: "there is no flaw in you."

It is as if this Bridegroom thought that the cynical world might think He was only mentioning her good features. He answers this by declaring her thoroughly beautiful and free from any defect.

Christ Jesus has no quarrel with His spouse. She often wanders from Him, grieving His Holy Spirit, but He does not allow her faults to affect His love. He sometimes corrects her, but it is always in the tenderest way, with the kindest intentions. He does not remember our foolish errors. He does not harbor grudges. He forgives us, and He loves us just as much after we sin as He does beforehand.

CHOSEN OF GOD

I have many people in this city.
Acts 18:10

This should be a great motivation for us to take God's message to those around us. Among the people in your city – among the sinful, the degraded, the drunken – God has people whom He has chosen to save.

When you take His Word to them, it means that God has chosen you to be the messenger of life to them. They must receive it, because God has chosen them to do so.

Even beyond this, these ungodly people are being prayed for before God's throne, by Christ Himself. Before long they will bend their stubborn knees and breathe their repentant sighs before the throne of grace. The chosen moment has not yet come for them. But when it comes, they will obey.

WHITER THAN SNOW

Ask and it will be given to you.
Matthew 7:7

Whenever a sinner is hungry, he only needs to knock, and his needs will be supplied. Whenever a soul is grimy and filthy, it can go there to be washed. The water is always flowing and it always cleanses. Sins that were scarlet and crimson have disappeared; sinners have been washed whiter than snow (Is. 1:18). The sinner merely needs to ask, and he will be clothed. Nothing that he needs will be denied. All these things are to be had by merely knocking at mercy's door.

Knock there this morning and ask for large things from your generous Lord. Do not leave the throne of grace until all your desires have been spread before the Lord. Don't let unbelief hinder you. Jesus invites you. Jesus has promised to bless you. Don't hold back.

ONE WITH CHRIST

As is the man from heaven,
so also are those who are of heaven.
1 Corinthians 15:48

Pause for a moment and think about this. Isn't it amazing how Christ could humble Himself to unite with such wretched souls as ours? Yet He lifts us into a glorious union with Himself. In Christ we are born with a new nature – God becomes our "Abba," our Father; Christ is our beloved brother.

Each one of us should be aware of our heritage; we should trace our lineage; we should take advantage of its privileges. We are one with Christ! In comparison, all earthly honors are empty.

LASTING LOVE

He chose the lowly things of this world.
1 Corinthians 1:28

Walk the streets by moonlight, if you dare, and you will see sinners then. Go wherever you want – you don't need to ransack the earth – sinners can be found in every street of every city, town, village, and hamlet. Jesus died for these people. In God's supreme love, He has chosen to turn some of the worst into the best. His redeeming love has invited many of the worst sinners to sit at the table of mercy. So there is always hope.

Think about Jesus' love. See His tearful eyes, His bloody wounds. This is love that streams out for you – strong, faithful, pure, and lasting love. This love doesn't care where you have been or what you have done. Just trust in Him and you will be saved.

ROBES OF RIGHTEOUSNESS

They will walk with me,
dressed in white, for they are worthy.
Revelation 3:4

We may see this as justification. That is, they will enjoy a constant sense of being right with God. They will understand that the righteousness of Christ has been put on their account and that they have been washed, made whiter than the new-fallen snow.

The one who is accepted by God wears white clothing of joy and gladness, and walks in sweet fellowship with Jesus.

Those who have not soiled their clothing here on earth will certainly walk in white in heaven, when the white-robed hosts sing eternal hallelujahs to the Most High God. They will have unspeakable joy and happiness they couldn't even dream of. They will walk with Christ in white because He has made them worthy.

UNANSWERED PRAYER

Therefore will the Lord wait,
that he may be gracious unto you.
Isaiah 30:18 KJV

God often delays in answering prayer. If you have been knocking at the gate of mercy and have received no answer, do you want to know why the Maker has not opened the door? Our Father has His own reasons for keeping us waiting.

Sometimes it is to show His power and sovereignty. More often, the delay is to our advantage. You may be kept waiting so that your desires will grow stronger. God knows that this will happen, and He may want you to see your need even more clearly, so you will appreciate His mercy, when it does come, all the more. Your prayers are all filed in heaven, and even if they are not answered immediately, they will not be forgotten. So don't lose hope. Keep praying.

WITH HIM FOREVER

And so we will be with the Lord forever.
1 Thessalonians 4:17

We can have occasional visits with Christ now, but oh, how short they are! We look forward eagerly to the time when we will see Him not at a distance, but face-to-face.

In heaven, our fellowship will not be interrupted by sin or by worries. It is so sweet to see Him, as we do, now and then – imagine what it will be like to be with Him forever! May that day come quickly.

We need not worry about the pain of death, because this sweet fellowship will make up for it. If dying means entering into uninterrupted communion with Jesus, then death truly is gain.

SECURE IN GOD

The one who calls you is faithful and he will do it.
1 Thessalonians 5:24

Heaven is a place where we will never sin. The wicked will not trouble us, and we will be able to rest. Heaven is the land of perfect holiness and complete security. But don't we on earth sometimes taste a bit of this security?

God's Word teaches us that all who are united to the Lamb are safe. Those who have committed their souls to Christ's keeping will find that He will preserve them faithfully.

I pray that God will convince you of your security in Christ. I pray that He will remind you that your name is engraved on His hands. I pray that you will hear Him whisper, "So do not fear, for I am with you" (Is. 41:10). He is bound by His perfect honor to present you before God's throne.

GOD'S WAYS

His ways are eternal.
Habakkuk 3:6

Human ways are variable. But God's ways are eternal. Things that He has done He will do again. The Lord's ways are the result of wise deliberation. He makes all things happen according to His own plans.

Nothing can take the Almighty by surprise. He has foreseen it all. God's ways are the outgrowth of His unchangeable character. His glorious attributes are clearly seen in His actions. He is just, gracious, faithful, wise, tender – and His actions are distinguished by the same traits. God is constant. He "does not change like shifting shadows" (Jas. 1:17).

It is not only His might that gives stability; His ways are the manifestation of the eternal principles of right. So go to God this morning with confidence. He is gracious to His people, and that will never change.

THE SALT OF GRACE

Salt without limit.
Ezra 7:22

Salt was used in every burnt offering made to the Lord. Due to its preserving and purifying properties, it became a symbol of God's grace in the soul. We can be quite sure that when the King of kings dispenses grace to His royal priests He does not cut short the supply. There is no limit on the salt of grace.

A person may have too much money, or too much honor, but he cannot have too much grace. To have God's gracious Spirit in overflowing proportions is to have fullness of joy.

So go to God's throne and get a large supply of heavenly salt. It will season your afflictions, preserve your heart, and kill your sins. You need a lot of it. Ask for it, and you'll get it.

DECEMBER 14

STRONGER THAN BEFORE

They go from strength to strength.
Psalm 84:7

These words convey the idea of progress. Those who rely on the Lord get stronger and stronger as they walk in the Lord's way. Usually, as we walk, we go from strength to weakness. We start fresh, well-prepared for the journey, but pretty soon the road becomes rough, and the sun grows hot, and we sit down by the roadside before plodding on.

But the Christian pilgrim obtains a fresh supply of grace along the way. He is as energetic after years of hard travel as he was when he started. He may not be quite as buoyant or bubbly; he may not burn with the same fiery zeal; but when it comes to real power, he is stronger than he ever was.

CLING TO JESUS

Then Orpah kissed her mother-in-law
good-by, but Ruth clung to her.
Ruth 1:14

It is one thing to love the ways of the Lord when things are easy and quite another to cling to them when it's difficult. The kiss of outward respect is cheap and easy, but clinging to the Lord, making that decision for truth and holiness, is no trifling matter.

Where do you stand? Is your heart clinging to Jesus? Have you counted the cost? Are you solemnly prepared to suffer loss in this world for the Master's sake? The reward will be substantial. Those who renounce everything else for Christ's sake will be blessed forever. Do not be satisfied this morning with a casual devotion to Christ. That is as empty as Orpah's kiss. By God's Holy Spirit, cling to Jesus.

COME AND FOLLOW

Come to me.
Matthew 11:28

This is the cry of the Christian religion: "Come." The gospel draws people with love. Jesus is the Good Shepherd, going before His sheep, calling them to follow Him, always leading them with the sweet word, "Come." From the first moment of your spiritual life to the time you are ushered into glory, this is what Christ says to you: "Come, come to Me."

He is always ahead of you, calling you to follow even as a soldier follows his captain. He goes before you to pave the way, to clear your path, and all your life you will hear His energizing voice. This is not only Christ's call to you, but this is what you say to Christ. You look forward to His second coming. "Come, Lord Jesus" (Rev. 22:20).

CHRIST REMEMBERS US

I remember the devotion of your youth.
Jeremiah 2:2

Christ loves to think about His church and to look on her beauty. We can never look too often on the face of someone we love. It is the same way with Jesus. From the beginning of time, He was "rejoicing in his whole world and delighting in mankind" (Prov. 8:31). His thoughts moved ahead to the time when His chosen ones would be born, seeing them through the glass of His foreknowledge.

As the names of Israel's tribes were written on the high priest's breastplate, so the names of Christ's chosen ones glitter like jewels upon His heart. We may often forget to think of our Lord, but He never ceases to remember us.

TRUE REPENTANCE

Rend your heart and not your garments.
Joel 2:13

Outward signs of religious emotion are easily done and frequently hypocritical. True repentance is much more difficult – and much less common. People will busy themselves with the most minute ceremonial regulations, because these things can make them proud of themselves, but heart-rending is divinely caused and solemnly felt.

It is a private grief that is personally experienced, not only in form, but deep within the believer's heart. It is powerfully humbling and completely sin-purging.

This text commands us to rend our hearts, but that is not easy. Our hearts are naturally hard as marble. We must take them to Calvary. The voice of our dying Savior has split rocks before (Mt. 27:50-51). It is just as powerful now.

WORTH MORE THAN SPARROWS

The lot is cast into the lap,
but its every decision is from the LORD.
Proverbs 16:33

If the Lord looks after even the casting of lots, don't you think He can arrange events in your life? Remember that the Savior has said that even sparrows will not fall without our Father's will.

It would bring you a holy calm, my friend, if you would remember this. It would relieve your anxiety, and you could live a patient, quiet, and cheerful life – as a Christian should. Hear the prayers of Jesus interceding for you, and ask yourself, "While He prays for me, will the Father ever act ungraciously toward me?" If He remembers sparrows, He won't forget you. "Cast your cares on the Lord and he will sustain you; he will never let the righteous fall" (Ps. 55:22).

ASSURED OF CHRIST'S LOVE

I have loved you with an everlasting love.
Jeremiah 31:3

Sometimes the Lord Jesus shares His loving thoughts with His people. He is wise enough to know when to hold back, but He often expresses His love clearly and announces it to the world. The Holy Spirit often confirms the love of Jesus, bearing witness with our spirit (Rom. 8:16 KJV). He takes the things of Christ and reveals them to us.

Ask the experienced Christians you know, and they will tell you that there have been times when they felt the love of Christ so clearly and certainly that to doubt it would be to doubt their own existence. Maybe you have enjoyed a closeness to the Lord that rules out any question of His affection for us. He wraps us in His embrace and squeezes our doubts out of us. Listen to His sweet voice. Be assured that He loves you with an everlasting love.

AN ETERNAL COVENANT

*Has he not made with me an everlasting
covenant, arranged and secured in every part?*
2 Samuel 23:5

This covenant is divine in its origin. God has
made it with us. Yes, God, the everlasting Father,
the God who spoke the world into existence,
stooped from His majesty, took hold of your
hand, and made a covenant with you. Isn't
that a remarkable deed? Can we ever really
understand the humbling that was involved in
that action?

It would be incredible enough if a human
king made an agreement with us. But the King
of all kings, El Shaddai, the All-sufficient Lord,
Yahweh of the ages – He has made an everlasting
covenant with us. The covenant is also eternal
in its duration. This is reassuring, amid all of
life's uncertainties, to know that "God's solid
foundation stands firm" (2 Tim. 2:19).

DECEMBER 22

ALL THE STRENGTH WE NEED

I will strengthen you.
Isaiah 41:10

God is certainly able to follow through on this promise. He has all the strength we need. The same God who keeps the earth in its orbit, who stokes the sun's furnace, who lights the stars of heaven, has promised to supply you with daily strength.

He created the world out of nothing; will He be unable to support His children? He holds back the thunderstorms, he rides on the wind, He holds the oceans in the palm of His hand – how can He fail you?

O God, my strength, I believe in Your promise. The limitless reservoir of Your strength can never be exhausted. Your overflowing storehouse will never be emptied. I can sing forever in Your strength.

DRAW CLOSE TO GOD

Friend, move up to a better place.
Luke 14:10

When our Christian life first begins, we draw close to God, but only with fear and trembling. At that point the soul is very conscious of its guilt. It reacts humbly, overawed by the Lord's grandeur. But in later life, as we grow in grace, we lose that sense of terror.

It's not that we forget our sin or that we lose our sense of holy awe in the presence of God. But our fear of God becomes a reverence, rather than a dread. We are called up to a "better place," with greater access to God through Christ. We see not only His greatness, but His love, His goodness, His mercy. We are aware of His limitless mercy and infinite love, and this refreshes us. We are invited to come to an even better position of closeness to God, rejoicing in Him and crying, "Abba, Father."

FOR YOUR SAKE

For your sakes he became poor.
2 Corinthians 8:9

The Lord Jesus Christ was eternally rich, glorified, and exalted. He could never have had fellowship with us unless He had shared with us His own abundant wealth, becoming poor to make us rich. If He had remained on His glorious throne and if we had stayed in the ruins of our sin, communion would have been impossible on both sides. The righteous Savior had to give His own perfection to His sinful brothers.

Giving and receiving in this way, He descended from His lofty position, and we rose from the depths.

Before a sinful soul can truly relate to the perfect God, it must lose its guilt and put on the righteousness of Christ. For your sake, the Lord Jesus "became poor," so that He could lift you into communion with Himself.

GOD WITH US

*The virgin will be with child and will give birth
to a son, and will call him Immanuel.*
Isaiah 7:14

Let's go today to Bethlehem, along with the marveling shepherds and the adoring magi, and see the one born King of the Jews. Jesus is Yahweh incarnate, our Lord and our God.

Let us adore and admire Him. Let us bow in reverence before this holy Child, whose innocence restores glory to humanity. And let us pray that He will be formed in us, as "the hope of glory" (Col. 1:27).

Immanuel, this Jesus, is "God with us" in our nature, our sorrow, our work, our punishment, even our death. He brings us with Him in His resurrection, ascension, triumph, and glory.

THE SECOND ADAM

The last Adam.
1 Corinthians 15:45

Jesus stands for every person He has chosen. Under the old agreement of works, Adam stood for every member of the human race. But under the new agreement of grace, every redeemed soul has a personal interest in Christ.

We are one with Him since He is the Second Adam, the Sponsor of every chosen soul in this new covenant of love.

Whatever Christ has done, He has done for the whole body of His church. We were crucified with Him and buried with Him (Col. 2:10-13), and, even more wonderful, we are risen with Him and ascended with Him to heavenly positions (Eph. 2:6).

Everything the Second Adam does is ours, too. Our salvation is based on this.

LIKE REEDS IN THE WIND

Can papyrus grow tall where there is no marsh?
Job 8:11

Papyrus is flimsy. So is the hypocrite. He has no substance or stability. The papyrus reed is shaken by every wind, just as the hypocrite yields to every outside influence. The papyrus reed thrives in the marshy ground. But if the marsh goes dry, the reed will wither. Its life is entirely dependent on circumstances.

Is this your situation, too? Do you only serve God when it is profitable or respectable to do so? Or can you honestly say that you have held on to your integrity when it has been inconvenient, even difficult to do so? Then there is genuine godly vitality in you. Plants that the Lord has planted can flourish even in the midst of drought. Those who follow Christ because they love Him, these are the ones He loves in a special way.

The Life of Christ

*The life I live in the body,
I live by faith in the Son of God.*
Galatians 2:20

Jesus' first command to us was "Live!" Life is absolutely essential in spiritual matters; until we have it, we have no way of participating in things of God's kingdom. What is this life that grace confers on us? It is none other than the life of Christ. Faith is the firstfruits of this transaction. Faith grabs hold of Jesus with a firm and determined grip. Christ Jesus is so delighted by faith that He keeps strengthening it and nurturing it in the believer, holding it in place with His eternal arms. So here we have pictured a living, logical, and delightful union that streams forth with love, confidence, sympathy, comfort, and joy. When you feel this oneness with Christ, you begin to sense your pulse beating with His.

MUCH, MUCH MORE

Thus far has the LORD helped us.
1 Samuel 7:12

The phrase "thus far" is like a hand pointing to the past. Through poverty and wealth, in sickness and health, at home and abroad, in trial and triumph, in prayer and temptation – "thus far the Lord has helped us!"

But the phrase also points forward. When someone reaches a certain point and says, "thus far," he is obviously not finished yet. There are more trials and joys, more prayers and answers, more labors, more strength, more victories – leading all the way to death. Is it over then? No! There is more – being made like Jesus, thrones, songs, white robes, Jesus' face, the company of believers, the glory of God, the infinite bliss. Thus far the Lord has proved Himself faithful, but there is much, much more to come.

A BETTER END

The end of a matter is better than its beginning.
Ecclesiastes 7:8

Look at our Lord's life. See how He began. "He was despised and rejected by men, a man of sorrows, and familiar with suffering" (Is. 53:3). But look how He ends up – at His Father's right hand, waiting in glory until His enemies are made His footstool (Lk. 20:42-43).

"In this world," writes John, "we are like him" (1 Jn. 4:17). You must bear the cross, too, or you will not wear the crown. You must wade through the mud, if you want to walk that golden pavement. So cheer up, if you find yourself in difficult straits. You are one of God's people. Let faith and patience fill your heart, for when your King is crowned, one perfect ray of glory will stream from you.

COME AND DRINK

*On the last and greatest day of the Feast,
Jesus stood and said in a loud voice, "If anyone
is thirsty, let him come to me and drink."*
John 7:37

On this last day of the year, Jesus pleads in the same way with us. He longs to show us His grace. His patience has been admirable, bearing with us year after year, despite our rebellions and resistance to His Spirit. Everything you need to quench your soul's thirst is here in Christ. For your conscience, the atonement brings peace. For your mind, the gospel brings rich instruction. For your heart, Jesus is the most worthy object of affection you could ever find.

Jesus gives an open invitation. Everyone who thirsts is welcome. There is no other qualification. You are not invited on the basis of your goodness. If you are thirsty, come and drink.